T0294017

DARYL
MITCHELL

with Frank Watson

DARYL MITCHELL

with Frank Watson

Once a Pear...
My Cricket Journey

Foreword by Moeen Ali

First published by Pitch Publishing, 2022

Pitch Publishing
9 Donnington Park,
85 Birdham Road,
Chichester,
West Sussex,
PO20 7AJ
www.pitchpublishing.co.uk
info@pitchpublishing.co.uk

ISBN 978 1 80150 202 3

Typesetting and origination by Pitch Publishing
Printed and bound in Great Britain by TJ Books, Padstow

CONTENTS

FOREWORD

by Moeen Ali

MITCH AND I played against each other a few times in county second XI cricket but it was when I joined Worcestershire in 2007 that our friendship really began. We quickly became more than just team-mates and his balanced, thoughtful views on all matters, not just cricket, meant that he was always my 'go-to guy' when I needed someone to talk to. For years we have shared countless sessions on the field or in the nets, hours in the dressing room and miles on the road. I can't think of anybody I'd rather have been alongside.

As a cricketer Mitch is one of those who certainly maximised his talents. His mental strength was an example to all and it was this toughness, as much as anything else, that allowed him to be the tremendously consistent performer that he was throughout his career. Mitch was one of my favourite people to bat with and I think we share the

7

view that we enjoyed a chemistry at the crease that enhanced both our games. I always considered Mitch to be one of the leading batsmen on the county circuit. I will always remember the game at Cheltenham in our promotion season of 2010 when he made a hundred in each innings to steer us to an important victory, a top class, totally professional performance. Of course, he also played many crucial knocks in one-day cricket and became the first ever bowler to take 100 wickets for Worcestershire in the Twenty20 format.

Mitch made a vital contribution to Worcestershire in his six years as captain. He led from the front and focused on other people, not just himself. His knowledge of the game is up there with the best of those that I've played with and I'd certainly say he's one of the best captains I've played under, and there have been a few!

Most importantly, though, Mitch is just a brilliant human being. He is massively loyal, generous, funny and just good to be around. It's no surprise that his fellow professionals elected him as chair of the PCA – the players' union – for the maximum two terms. There couldn't have been anybody better to represent their interests.

It's always difficult to assess a player's overall contribution to a county club when comparing those from different eras. Clearly there have been some wonderful players in Worcestershire's history and in my opinion Mitch has to go down as one of the county's finest. It is not easy to be as consistent a performer at the top of the order as he was, facing the new ball day in and day out, often in difficult conditions. I suppose the single biggest compliment I can pay him is to say, quite honestly, when I think of Worcestershire I think of Mitch.

1

CLOSE OF PLAY

IT WASN'T how I'd planned it. I'd always had a hopeful vision of my career ending on something of a high. Perhaps my club, Worcestershire – the Pears – would win some silverware that year. Perhaps, after a season of heavy run-scoring, my final innings would be followed by a walk from the middle of Worcestershire's New Road ground to the appreciation of a packed pavilion allowing me to share the moment with county members, many of whom I'd known for the best part of two decades. I might even have finished with a hundred. But if there's one thing I learned in my time in the game, it's that reality very rarely matches imagination. Generally speaking, I believe, you get what you earn and in professional sport that's absolutely true.

My playing days actually drew to a close on a warm September evening at the end of the 2021 season, the second in consecutive years to be hugely affected by the Covid-19 pandemic. New Road was sparsely populated and the pavilion closed to the public. Though we had won that final game, against Leicestershire, in three days, the victory was not particularly significant. It brought to an end a hugely disappointing season for Worcestershire which had seen us promise much but deliver little. Personally, I had underachieved.

That isn't to say that I was unappreciative of the generous send-off that I received from those that were present, be they players, journalists, staff or spectators. The Leicestershire team had given me a 'guard of honour' as I made my way out to bat in the first innings and the club had made me a memorable presentation during the lunch interval on that last day. When I did make my final walk back to the empty pavilion, having scored 9 not out as we made the 12 runs needed for a 10-wicket victory, those elsewhere in the ground stood in lengthy applause and I was pleased that my parents, wife and children were there. It was real and it was deeply meaningful but it wasn't the stuff of boyhood dreams.

It had been a strange few weeks. Having not qualified for the latter rounds of either of the two domestic white ball competitions we had finished in the bottom two of our group in the County Championship's first stage and been placed in Division Three for the second part. This meant that we had four games at the end of the season which, in all honesty, were of limited consequence. Of course, as professional county cricketers, all players have a responsibility to apply themselves whatever the circumstances but when there is little riding on results it can be difficult to reach maximum levels of motivation. That might depend, of course, on a particular player's circumstances; a youngster in his first two or three seasons might well be highly driven in any first-class game, a veteran opening batsman who's already made the decision to retire perhaps less so!

It was made clear to me that I didn't have to play in all of those remaining games but even entering the last few weeks of my career, the idea of voluntarily not representing Worcestershire went very much against the grain. I had dedicated my entire professional life to the Pears and I wasn't going to quit early. Also, one was against Middlesex at Lord's and the opportunity to play at 'the home of cricket' just once more was welcome. I might even get a hundred! There I go, dreaming again! In reality, on a seamer-friendly surface, I failed to reach double figures in my last two innings at Lord's, and indeed throughout those last four games never really got myself 'in' at any time.

Retirement and the transition out of a playing career had been in my mind for some time. I had finished my second two-year stint as chair of the Professional Cricketers'

Association in February 2021 and taken up a part-time role as the PCA's director of cricket operations, knowing that when my playing days ended the position would become full-time. If I had written my own script, that change would have occurred at the end of the 2022 season but events during 2021 dictated otherwise.

I didn't score the runs that I should have in Championship cricket and I was disappointed that I wasn't given more opportunity in the Twenty20 games, especially once Moeen Ali had become unavailable after a brief spell at the beginning of the competition. I was especially frustrated to be left out of two consecutive matches that we lost on the road at Trent Bridge and Headingley. However, I was satisfied with the outcome of some honest conversations with head coach, Alex Gidman, and accepted that the club wanted me to focus on the red-ball game for the remaining time, perhaps only making the odd contribution in shorter formats. The thinking was that there were young players coming through who could and should be able to fulfil the sort of role that I had previously.

I agreed, accepting that I would, going forward, be almost exclusively a red-ball player. With that proviso the coaches wanted me to play for another year and I was happy to do so, hopefully looking forward to a final season, a 20th with the Pears, played in a non-Covid environment.

That changed when it came to discussing a new contract about six weeks or so before the end of the season. I was disappointed with the terms offered to me and could not reach an agreement with the hierarchy. In short, I would be significantly better off retiring and if that offer reflected my perceived value to the club it was definitely time to move on.

So it was that my transition into a full-time role at the PCA was advanced by a year. Whilst that was not what I might have planned, I can have no animosity towards Worcestershire. I had a brilliant 19 years at the club, 17 of them in the first team, and as those final few weeks unfolded I became increasingly comfortable with my decision. I was also acutely aware of my privileged position in terms of having a future career in place, and therefore being able to look forward without fear or immediate financial concern, a luxury not many retiring sportsmen enjoy. As my PCA work has clearly demonstrated to me, many professional sportsmen reach the end of their playing careers with limited employment prospects.

I have asked myself whether or not knowing that I had my future so securely mapped out might have just taken the edge off my hunger in terms of run-scoring in my last season and the truth is I don't know. I cannot deny that I was no longer playing for my future and whether or not subconsciously that detracted from my performance, I honestly can't say. What I do know is that I never knowingly gave anything less than my best even though there were a couple of occasions in that last season when I found myself really struggling in the middle.

Another way in which I am fortunate, I think, is that I can say I reflect on my career with no regrets. It has been suggested that I might have played for England but I find that one easy to deal with; it wasn't my call so it is pointless to worry about it. I don't think I could have done much more than I did in terms of maximising my talent. I know that my name was discussed in at least two England selection meetings and I did allow myself to become genuinely hopeful during the 2015 Ashes series. At that time I was top of the Division One County Championship averages and Adam Lyth was struggling opening the batting against the Aussies, but the selectors stuck with him and actually my own season tailed off a little bit.

Generally, though, I'm not a character that deals in regret, believing that you make your choices and you live with them. I adopt the same attitude, I suppose, when I reflect on turning down opportunities to move to a different county. At various points in my career I could have moved, and I could have hugely improved my salary by doing so, but such decisions are particularly difficult for a local family man. One very attractive option with which I was presented came not long after the birth of our second child and shortly after being removed from the Worcestershire captaincy. After discussing everything with my wife, Danni, and other members of the family, we made a collective decision that I should stay. Cricketers spend enough time in hotels anyway, and if we hadn't uprooted the family I'd have been practically living in one! Had the domestic situation been different, who knows?

That said, the ties that bind me still to Worcestershire are incredibly strong and whilst I don't look back with regret, I do look back with immense pride at having represented the county of my birth with distinction for such a long time. Winning the Twenty20 Blast in 2018, undoubtedly the high point of my career, was an unforgettable experience and in some ways I regard it as a single, shining reward for my loyalty. A trophy with the Pears undoubtedly meant more to me, my friends and my family than any success I might have achieved elsewhere.

That last game against Leicestershire had finished on a Thursday and there followed a busy weekend of end-of-season activities including informal dressing room beers, a surprise retirement bash arranged by the lads, and the annual Players' Awards Evening. Therefore, there hadn't been much time for the significance of the events of the past few days to really sink in before I went to New Road on the last Monday in September to empty my locker. As I arrived at the ground I bumped into a couple of the young lads, Dillon Pennington and Jack Haynes, both at the opposite end of their careers from me, but when I reached the dressing room I found it deserted.

That's perhaps when it actually became real to me that I was no longer a Worcestershire player. I sat in my usual place in the corner of the room by the window for a long time and I can't really remember my exact thoughts. I did reflect on how different those facilities in the Graeme Hick pavilion at New Road were from those we had in the old pavilion in my early years. Back then, the younger players changed in a different room almost up in the roof space and it was only when you had established yourself as a first team regular that you were allowed downstairs. We even had to knock on the door to gain access to the big boys! I recall not even daring to walk through the senior dressing room on the way to the nets but having to go around the back of the pavilion to use the rear staircase.

By the end of my playing career, things had become very different for the younger players coming into the game and rightly so. Nonetheless, back then there was some value in being aware of your appropriate place in the grand scheme and I do wonder if the increasing lack of patience in the modern digital world has impacted negatively on young people generally. The increased emphasis on how things look, and the instantaneous nature of a life where information is literally at your fingertips via whichever mobile device you use, has made all of us become less able to bide our time, and young sportsmen are no different. They want instant recognition, high profiles, big salaries and, given how the world of social media has shaped them, this is understandable.

Early in my career, it was simply the numbers on the scorecard which mattered and though that will ultimately always remain the case in a game like cricket, the exaggerated perception that the way things look is paramount has made life more complicated for the new generation. It has become harder for coaches to keep players happy and the increasing involvement of agents pushing the interests of their charges has exacerbated the situation.

An empty cricket dressing room is an interesting space, filled with memories but also with potential; which great players have celebrated or agonised here and who will follow? What triumphs and disasters have been experienced and which lie ahead? I can't say that I recalled certain days or moments as I sat there but it was a special and quite emotional experience and I became lost in thought. I did consider that I might never go into that room again. I took down the pictures of my kids that decorated my locker, packed up those items of kit which I wanted to keep and threw out some old stuff. I left various bits and pieces out for others to make use of and, unable to resist one last practical joke, I removed all the grips from Jack Haynes's collection of bats and signed them all, with an accompanying message, on the face. He'd attempted to prank me (poorly) a couple of times down at Lord's and, as the experienced professional, I had to have what would literally be the last laugh.

Such silliness, fun and frivolity are perhaps what I miss most after retirement. That jocular aspect of life as a professional in a team sport is hugely important. Cricketers probably spend more time together than players in any other game. There are the many practice sessions, the travelling, the time spent in hotels as well as the long hours playing the game. It's vitally important to commit to the team ethic, to understand the dressing room mood, to engage with it and to play your part in making it work. I can't even begin to quantify the extent to which my adult self has been shaped by my experiences in various dressing rooms around the world. I wouldn't say I've changed fundamentally – I'm still that kid from the Vale of Evesham who entered a very different professional cricket world at the start of the millennium – but almost everything I've learned has been because of the people I've played alongside.

My relatively sheltered youth meant that I was unacquainted with a variety of cultures and backgrounds when I embarked upon my cricket career. Everything I've come to understand about Hinduism came from Vikram Solanki, and about Islam from Moeen Ali. Asking other people questions and learning to appreciate the way they see the world and not just how they play cricket has helped me to become a more rounded individual than I might otherwise have been. It's obvious that such development might have happened whatever profession I had pursued but for me it's been in a cricket context.

Seeing other players struggle with periods of bad form and come through it, observing those reaching the end of their careers and dealing with it, recognising when people have made mistakes in terms of behaviour and how they've responded have all been contributory elements of my personal growth which are attributable to cricket and the dressing room environment. I've also been able, through cricket, to travel the world and to spend time in many countries I might not otherwise have visited, to mix with and play alongside people from a huge variety of geographical, cultural, educational and economic backgrounds, all again vitally important in shaping the person I have become.

I'm not usually a particularly emotional person and I had coped fairly well with the events of that last week or two, unlike my mum who had been very moved, especially during the last game. However, as I sat there on that Monday morning the tears weren't far away. Had I taken one of those opportunities to play elsewhere, I never would have felt like that. I wondered how many players beginning at county level would ever spend so many years at one club. In a changing cricket landscape of franchises, loans and routine transfers, the likelihood of spending an entire career wearing one badge was receding. How many future players would, like I did, play in all versions of the game? The global impact of shorter forms of cricket and the potentially life-changing sums which players can earn by focusing on the white ball has seen the likelihood of players of my type – a home-grown, one-club man playing in all formats – decrease significantly. And that's not to make a value judgement of any kind whatsoever, just to recognise the evolution of the game.

I also stood on the pavilion balcony for a long time and just took in my surroundings. Considered, I suppose, to be amongst the most famous in cricket, the view across to Worcester Cathedral simply never loses its appeal and players appreciate that too. I knew I would miss it and though I'd come to the ground as a spectator in future, it wouldn't look quite the same as it did from the dressing room. I strolled out to the middle of the ground to give one of my playing shirts to the groundsman, Tim Packwood, as a gift to his son and on the walk back I took one last look at the ground from the inside, so to speak. I can't properly describe my feelings at that point; there were probably just too many to process.

I put my stuff in the car and climbed back up the stairs for one last time. When we were replacing some furniture at home a few years earlier I had brought an old sofa in to make the dressing room a bit more comfortable and as I took a final glance through the door I remember thinking, 'That's my sofa.'

I decided to leave it.

2

FINDING A WAY

'A STUBBORN, opinionated smart-arse' is what my former opponent, team-mate and later coach, Alan Richardson, once called me.

And though he did go on to qualify his judgement by stating that such personal qualities were 'perfect attributes for an opening batsman in professional cricket', his apparently less than complimentary assessment probably does hint at those aspects of my character which have served me well in my sporting life. I noticed during a recent read of my 2016 benefit brochure that several of my team-mates referenced my obsession with 'always finding a way' whether the contest be a game of county cricket, competitive winter batting drills or dressing room darts. I certainly don't dispute such observations. To put it simply, I like winning and hate losing.

I've lost count of the number of times I've been asked what I consider to be the attributes which made me the cricketer I was. In all honesty I'd have to say that they are the same qualities which have underpinned all areas of my life since I can remember. Yes, I do hate coming second but there's a bit more to it than that. I've always felt that those who do best in any field are those who make the most of what they've got to work with. Whether it be getting ready for an examination, a business meeting or a cricket match, it pays to prepare thoroughly, to have a clear plan and to stick to it within reason.

My drive to win was probably instilled in me by my father, Keith. Although he was only a good village cricketer, also an opening batsman, I spent many hours watching him occupy the crease for Badsey in the Cotswold Hills League and whether or not I realised it at the time I was, even then, learning the value of simply not getting out. It became clear to me that it was a lot more fun batting than sitting at the side watching somebody else! Dad wasn't a dashing strokemaker but he stuck around and made his fair share of runs. Whenever we played any game, be it garden cricket, pool, darts or table tennis, he never deliberately let me win. It just wasn't in his nature. In that sense, he brought me up to be tough, certainly not to expect to be given an easy ride in any sporting contest, and though some might regard that approach as overly harsh, I genuinely believe it was a benefit to me that I reaped long into adulthood. And, believe me, once it reached the point where, on the odd occasion, I started to beat Dad, I relished it and eagerly grabbed any opportunity!

Since becoming a father myself, I have, of course, considered my own role in such a context. With my children I have tried to steer a middle way and perhaps have not been as tough with them as Dad was with me. That said, I have no complaints. In fact, I'd go as far as to say that without me even realising it, those early lessons that taught me not to expect any free gifts when it came to winning were crucial in shaping the sportsman, and especially the cricketer, that I became.

That process which defined my sporting identity was also developed as a result of my early recreational experiences. For some reason, I always seemed to be the youngster playing with the older lads. I was playing men's cricket at 12 years of age and men's football at 14. In those environments, you just learned to grow up fast and to be honest I think the culture was a little tougher then than perhaps it had become by the end of my time as a professional. Even in those amateur teams, the ethos was all about winning and, youngster or not, you had to learn to take it on the chin when a bit of criticism came your way after a less than satisfactory performance.

I remember being in the firing line quite a lot in those early days and I think it forced me to grow up pretty quickly. As a teenager, I was welcome to join the older lads for a beer whether after cricket or football, but the price you paid for inclusion in the group was that you had to accept the brickbats as well as the plaudits. I've been on the wrong end of many a 'sledge' in professional cricket but I honestly don't think any of them even compare to some of the things I've been called in the changing room or bar at Bretforton Sports Club!

I suppose, then, that the need to find a way to win, which many of my Worcestershire colleagues have identified as one of my most characteristic traits, became almost instinctive. When I was still a small boy, and owing to Mum's work commitments, my sister, Kate, and I spent most Sundays at my grandmother's house. Gran was a wonderful companion and a very patient back garden bowler. And she certainly needed to be because, weather permitting, I was even then prepared to bat all day! Kate, the lone fielder, usually got bored and went indoors after about an hour. I think I once racked up a score of about 756 before missing one and then proceeded to clean bowl Gran first ball before choosing not to enforce the follow-on and digging in again! To get a four in that particular garden, you had to hit the house roughly in the direction of mid-wicket and I often think that was where I learned to become proficient in that area, working the ball in front of square on the leg side.

Similarly, when, as a 10- or 11-year-old, I regularly played with the older lads outside at Bretforton, the side of the pavilion counted as a boundary and, given the situation of the makeshift pitch we played on, for me that meant steering the ball down to third man. I don't actually know how many of my nearly 14,000 first-class runs were scored in that area but it was a fair percentage – as I'm sure dozens of disgruntled seamers up and down the country will testify! As a smallish boy in my early teens, I was never able to smash the ball around the park so I learned that to be successful, through sheer necessity, I had to learn to stick around, to play long innings and grind people down, to work the ball into areas where I could score. The truth is that never really changed; even at the end of my career I was essentially the same kind of player.

I can't claim to be the only sportsman, amateur or professional, who is ultra-competitive, though. As I have said, my father was the same, and obviously there are thousands of others who hate losing, some perhaps a lot more than me! However, I suppose what is striking about that observation regarding a desire to win when related to my own character is that it's been regularly made by other professionals. Clearly, they have seen in me a drive, perhaps almost an obsession with winning that goes beyond what they normally come across.

In all honesty, I have to acknowledge that there must be an element of selfishness involved; I think deep down all batters are selfish to some extent. John Arlott once wrote that cricket 'is called a team game but, in fact, no one is so lonely as a batsman facing a bowler supported by ten fieldsmen' and looked at that way, batting has to be a selfish business. Once you reach a certain level in the game – call it, say, serious cricket – all batsmen care about their statistics, and if they tell you otherwise they're either not very good or not entirely honest. Of course, there are times when you sacrifice your wicket for the cause, in a desperate run chase for example, but by and large you know you are judged on performance and that means how many runs you've made.

When you're a professional, whose entire livelihood depends upon those runs, it's almost impossible not to be at least in some part selfish when it comes to batting. It's very easy to sit at the side of a ground and criticise a batsman for apparently playing for himself or scoring too slowly but if you were able to put yourself in his position, to understand his mindset at that particular time, your judgement might be different. Sometimes, a batsman may be aware that he needs a score to keep his place in the side. Another might be aware that he is being considered for international selection and one more good innings might further enhance his claims. A young player might be trying to establish himself in a team, or maybe force his way up the order. Who wouldn't be selfish in such circumstances? Indeed, perhaps selfishness is a desirable quality.

That doesn't mean I never tried to help other players and certainly when I was captain of Worcestershire I regarded that as central to the role. In my PCA work, first as the county club's representative and then as chair, concern for the issues faced by others was clearly the focus, so the ability to compartmentalise my life became crucial. Indeed, that very skill – learning to separate different aspects of one's life – is something I have attempted to teach to others as I consider it especially useful in dealing with the day-to-day pressures of a life in professional sport.

Handling failure is a huge part of being a successful batsman. To illustrate that I need to look no further than what was probably my most successful season in first-class cricket in 2017. That year, I made 1,266 runs at an average of 55.55. However, that included seven hundreds and three fifties in 26 innings. In 12 of those innings, I was dismissed for fewer than ten runs and I recorded four other scores of 30 or fewer. Accepting low scores as part of the deal of being a top order professional batsman is, in my opinion, vital and without it, a player is liable, as many have, to suffer all sorts of anguish and even to experience some mental health difficulties.

I was never a bat thrower, one of those characters whose dismissals led their team-mates to vacate the dressing room in anticipation of a volcanic outburst. For me, it was a case of sitting down for a few minutes to evaluate what had happened then taking off my batting gear, putting on a tracksuit, getting a cup of tea and moving on. Occasionally I might have chucked a glove into my kit bag if I thought I'd suffered a bad decision but that was probably the total of any tangible demonstration of my anger. From quite an early stage in my career I was able to take the view that once I was out, there was nothing I could do about it, other than to look at what happened to see if there was perhaps something I could work on technically to prevent the same thing happening again. By the end of my time as a player, analysis had become so high-tech that being able to look closely at a dismissal on video quickly after the event was very easy, whereas early on in my career it was more a process of self-reflection and perhaps a conversation with a coach or team-mate.

I clearly remember when I first heard a top player talk about the need to 'stay level' – to develop the ability to keep both success and failure in perspective. It seems to have become part of every coach's thinking in more modern times but the idea that you shouldn't get too high when things go well or too low when they don't, wasn't really something I was told as a youngster. The realisation came when, as a 21-year-old, I was doing 12th man duties for England in the third Ashes Test match at Old Trafford in 2005.

I was determined to take in the whole experience and to glean from it anything I could which might help my development. Andrew Strauss had made a hundred in the second innings only for Kevin Pietersen to be dismissed first ball immediately after. I was struck by the fact that had somebody walked into the dressing room at that point they would not have been able to say which man had made a century and which had bagged a first baller! I later overheard a conversation on the pavilion balcony in which Strauss emphasised to the coach, Duncan Fletcher, his belief that things are rarely as good or as bad as they seem, and from that day it was a mantra that stuck with me throughout my career.

Obviously, staying true to such a philosophy cuts both ways; it's not going to work for you if you get carried away by success and believe you're a wonderful player only to dismiss failure as inconsequential or, worse still, to blame it on others or make excuses. That way, I believe, leads to arrogance. Rather, for me, it translated into an attitude which meant that when I scored a hundred, I would think, 'Well that's my job. I should be making big runs,' whilst remaining totally aware that in my next innings I could well be dismissed for a low score.

Equally, when I did fail, I could think that there was no need to be overly upset and believe that my next innings was another chance to post a substantial score. Moeen Ali, one of my closest friends in the game, was one of the finest examples of this approach that I have ever encountered. He might have scored 150 or 0 and honestly, if you encountered him shortly after his dismissal, you simply would not be able to tell. Another benefit of such stoicism is that if you can practise it successfully, you are less likely to allow indifferent performances on the field to impact on your home life. The last thing a wife wants when she's had a busy day with the kids is a grumpy husband crashing through the front door complaining about a bad lbw decision!

Underpinning those aspects of my personality which drove me towards cricketing success was what I like to consider as a reasonably strong work ethic. Of course, attitudes towards physical fitness and its impact on performance changed hugely over the course of my career. In my first few years in the county game, the culture was much more relaxed regarding socialising before and during games than it later became. Some players would enjoy a few beers or glasses of wine during the evening even if they had

'ONCE A PEAR ...'

to play the following day. Certain away trips might be more eagerly anticipated than others because of the nightspots you might visit in that town.

In terms of practice, things were also quite flexible; some players were enthusiastic trainers and took every opportunity for net sessions whilst others preferred just to have a few throwdowns before the day's play or, in the case of a bowler, simply to bowl a few leisurely deliveries here and there. Make no mistake, many of those who followed such regimes were still absolutely top-class cricketers and performed to a high standard throughout very successful careers.

But times change and the growing attention to detail in all areas of elite performance absolutely revolutionised the approach to the job of almost every county cricketer. The introduction of 12-month contracts meant that clubs quite rightly had much more control over their employees than previously. The application of sports science, the introduction of strength and conditioning coaches, dieticians and sports psychologists, as well as specialist coaches for specific in-game disciplines, all impacted significantly in a few short years and the game was better for it.

Personally, I feel fortunate that I always quite enjoyed training, and running in particular. I am not for a minute suggesting that in my early days as a professional I didn't take opportunities to have a beer or two, and indeed I'd

34

say that a great deal of what I learned about the game in those first few formative years was learned over a glass. But I always felt that there was a time and a place and that you had to pay your dues – in other words, if you did indulge yourself in the bar you had to put a bit of extra effort into the next training session.

Even in my later playing days I relished the chance to beat the youngsters in any bleep tests or time trials we used to be put through, showing them that the old man still had what it took. By then I had learned a great deal, too, about diet and hydration for example, which helped me, along with my natural competitive spirit, to keep on finding a way to win, to keep on making the most of what I still regard as my relatively limited ability when compared to many others. Preparation was always the key for me; if I had done all I could ahead of the game the outcome would look after itself. That's where my confidence came from and what allowed me to 'stay level'.

Several different sports psychologists were employed by Worcestershire at various times during my playing days and some, like Dave Young and Chris Marshall, I found to be particularly helpful whilst there were others with whom I didn't connect especially well. One of the latter, Steve Sylvester was, I know, a great help to Moeen Ali. It is a purely individual thing and understandably so. Some of my team-mates benefited most from those that I found less useful and vice-versa. What I always tried to do was to listen and to be receptive because in such matters you never really know who is going to be best placed to help unless you give them a chance.

I tried to develop what I called a filter so that I could retain what I considered useful but let go of ideas I found unhelpful or confusing. As I gained experience, I became much better at knowing what would or would not help me. Like a lot of batsmen, I found the ability to 'switch off' between deliveries became a vital skill for me and various psychologists helped with that. I also found useful some of the advice I received regarding concentration and staying 'in the present' by regulating my breathing. It was often reassuring to find that many of the habits and routines which I had developed for myself were broadly what the experts were recommending!

I adopted a similar approach when it came to the various coaches whose guidance I received at different times. Some were especially helpful, others less so, but I always tried to listen, to be coachable and to keep learning. I found it possible to improve by gleaning information from other players, too, by keeping an open mind and by being constantly receptive to new ideas. I'd have to say I probably picked up a lot of useful advice in hotel bars as well, or perhaps in the bar at

New Road having a beer after the game with opposition players or coaches.

Damian D'Oliveira was probably my greatest mentor and certainly knew my game better than anybody. He had a priceless ability to watch me for just a few minutes in the nets and see if something was slightly wrong with my batting. I can hardly remember him bowling or throwing a ball at me, but he would frequently put me back on track with a brief but astute observation such as 'You're falling over a bit, Mitch. Remember to keep your head going towards mid-on.' That's my kind of technical coaching – clear and simple.

All the fitness training, psychological input and working with coaches is part of the process of correct preparation to which I referred earlier, a concept which I consider to be almost a transferable skill. I have always tried as far as possible to be appropriately prepared for whatever task I am faced with even in areas of my life outside cricket. I have found this especially important in my work for the PCA where it always pays to be up to speed and abreast of whatever details surround an issue of concern.

However, I'm not sure that my friends and family would describe me as a particularly well-organised character in my personal life. In dealing with more mundane matters, I tend to be more relaxed, and though I'll eventually get things done, when it comes to everyday chores I might need someone like my wife to present me with a list first! It's probably best summed up by saying that if I can recognise a clear outcome or target, I will approach a task in an organised and measured fashion. For example, I will happily cook anything provided I have a clear recipe and all the necessary ingredients laid out in front of me!

Another aspect of being a successful batsman which can be traced back to the essential elements of a person's character is bravery. I've never regarded myself as especially courageous but others have said to me that it must be a given if someone is to face up to the quickest bowlers day in, day out and I suppose that's the case. I was fortunate that throughout my career I was never really badly hit by a fast bowler and probably the worst I suffered were two or three glancing blows on the helmet. Remarkably, I never broke a finger or thumb either which, I think, is quite unusual for someone who played for as long as I did.

Word soon gets around the county circuit if there are suspicions that a player 'doesn't fancy it' when faced with short-pitched fast bowling and I'd like to think that I was never the subject of such conversations! I never actually feared a particular bowler because of his pace. In fact, I think I probably preferred a bit of pace on the ball to bowling of a more gentle variety. Most batsmen will tell you that what they really fear is what we call 'dibbly-dobblers' – those purveyors of gentle medium pace to whom getting out is a real sin. Just ask any of my own 33 first-class victims!

That's not to say that I wasn't ever discomforted by the quick stuff but merely to recognise that any fear I had was a fear of getting out rather than of getting hit. One occasion that springs to mind immediately is a game we played against Sussex at Hove in 2017. Jofra Archer bowled with a lot of pace and hostility on what cricketers call an 'up and down' pitch, basically a surface of variable bounce, and though I made a hundred in the first innings and shared an opening partnership of 220 with Brett D'Oliveira, we both felt that we could have been 'badged' at any stage. Jofra hit me (and hurt me!) under the armpit with two successive deliveries just before tea on the second day and Chris Jordan also bowled some fiery stuff. As we had our usual mid-pitch chats between overs, Dolly and I were both laughing, and secretly praying for the slightly less hostile Vernon Philander to be introduced into the attack so that we could throw our hands at a bit of 75mph outswing!

There's a part of such encounters that you love as a batter because that's when the adrenaline really gets pumping and it's important to enjoy it, genuinely to have a bit of fun out there, too. I honestly remember both Brett and myself chuckling at the non-striker's end as another rocket from Jofra went flying past the other's nose! Of course, we were urging each other to be alert and to watch the ball carefully but there was certainly a degree of humour involved. Another, perhaps slightly strange, perspective I take when considering such experiences is that not many people ever get such opportunities so you might as well make the most of them.

And, of course, wherever possible, find a way.

3

BRET BOY

I WAS born in Badsey, a village just outside Evesham, but when I was two years old my family moved just a mile or so to a house in the same village, just on Bretforton Road, which was to be my home until I became a permanent member of the Worcestershire playing staff. Bretforton – or 'Bret' as it's known to the locals – lies firmly in the Vale of Evesham in south-east Worcestershire, and is one of England's foremost fruit- and vegetable-growing regions. Sitting on the very edge of the Cotswolds it is in many ways as traditional a Worcestershire village as it is possible to imagine. In those days, agriculture was at the heart of the community, providing employment for a good percentage of those who lived there and with its village hall, garage, pub and sports club, Bretforton was a place whose customs had been in existence for generations.

As a youngster, of course, I was unaware of any of that but have since come to appreciate the extent to which my life was shaped by my environment in those early years. Many of my lifelong friends, those whom I will always class as my best mates, are from the village and still live in and around the area, and wherever I have been or will go in the future, it will always be the place I really regard as home. The fact that I came from such a long-established rural background and went on to captain my county on the cricket field is a source of great pride and has, perhaps subconsciously, always underpinned my personal appraisal of my career.

I now know that when I was appointed to the Worcestershire captaincy late in the 2010 season, I was the first player born within the county to hold that position since Maurice Foster in 1925. Whilst that might seem insignificant in the modern age of international travel and global cricket, it remains special to me and my family and, I believe, does resonate with many members of the club. I have been told that during my final game at Lord's in 2021 a BBC commentator, who was working for Middlesex, referred to me as 'Mr Worcestershire' and though that might have been something of a throwaway remark to him, it meant a lot to me!

My memories of that rural childhood don't go much further than my involvement with sport. From as early an age as I can remember, my life revolved around cricket, football and, in my years of secondary education, rugby. When I wasn't playing sport, I was either watching it or thinking about it, though I wouldn't say I can ever recall making a conscious decision that I wanted to make a living from it. I think a fair summary of my school reports, right from my days at Badsey First School, through to Prince Henry's High School in Evesham via Blackminster Middle School, would be to say that I did just enough to get by in terms of academic commitment.

Though I wouldn't class myself as a scholar, I had some ability in maths and science subjects and quite enjoyed geography. Subjects with a statistical aspect always appealed more to me than those like English and history which had a rather wordier bent. In keeping with my approach to sport, I always tended to take a somewhat pragmatic stance, tending to ask, 'What do I have to do to successfully reach the next stage?' Helped by the fact that Prince Henry's was a good school with a solid academic ethos, I was able to summon up the necessary focus to achieve the requisite GCSE grades to move into the sixth form and to pass my A levels in geography, psychology and PE which ideally qualified me to read sports science at university.

During those school years, though, it's probably fair to say that I was certainly more concerned with my sporting development than what was going on in the classroom. Growing up in the Vale it was almost inevitable that when it came to football, despite my father's allegiance to Chelsea owing to his London roots, I would become an Aston Villa fan. Villa have a large following in that part of Worcestershire and most of my mates were supporters. So I was excited when, after attending a summer football school, I was invited to become part of the club's youth programme and for three years attended training sessions in Worcester on Friday nights and then on Sunday mornings at the Villa training complex at Bodymoor Heath. The fact that one of the perks of involvement was the provision of free tickets for home games was an added bonus! It was quite a thrill to put on the claret and blue shirt and to be coached by club legends like Gary Shaw and Peter Withe, but I was quickly aware that in terms of ability, I was in the lower echelons of the group and I was not especially surprised that I was eventually not retained as part of the ongoing squad.

I was introduced to rugby union at middle school and this grew into something more significant when I moved on to Prince Henry's. Here, I found rugby was taken seriously and the structured programme put together by two of the teachers in particular, John Cox and Tim Hoban, appealed very much to my ambitious teenage self. Not surprisingly, given my mindset, I set about finding a way to get myself into the team which was largely comprised of boys with much more rugby experience than me. As a fairly talented footballer, and with decent hands because of my cricket experience, I realised that I had some adaptable skills and managed to force my way into the side, firstly at full-back and later at outside-half.

We enjoyed some very successful years and had a couple of lengthy cup runs and triumphs, during which we beat some much more established rugby schools. What I most enjoyed about that involvement was the training, the organisation and the planning that went into achieving success. Perhaps, without realising, I was again learning lessons which would come to fruition in later years. For a few of those teenage years, my winter sporting commitments were probably excessive and I doubt that many contemporary physical educationalists would regard it as sensible that as a 14- or 15-year-old I would play school rugby on a Saturday morning before playing football in the afternoon for Bretforton then on a Sunday two more football matches, one for Bret and one for Badsey Colts!

It was still cricket, though, which commanded most of my attention. Dad moved as a player from Badsey to Bretforton when I was 12 and I played a couple of games for the club on a Sunday that year. The following season, Bret began to operate a second XI and that was probably a highly significant decision in terms of my own opportunities. I made my first fifty for the club in men's cricket aged 13 at Inkberrow in quite amusing circumstances. I was due to bat at No.3 as we chased a target of about 240 but one of the designated openers, Ant Clarke, was caught short and had to go to the lavatory just before the innings began! I was therefore promoted in the order and proceeded, along with my partner, Andrew Witt, to knock off the runs for a ten-wicket victory. I finished 80-odd not out and was aware that I had passed something of a milestone.

I was playing regularly, too, for the Bret Under-16 side that my father organised and I stayed in the second team the following season. On reflection, this was good management from the club as there might have been a temptation to throw me into the first XI too soon. I suspect Dad might have had some input there! In the seconds, I was able to open the batting every week and also to bowl my full allocation of ten overs in most games so in terms of my development it was a much better option. In that second season, aged 14, I scored four hundreds and was thus a far more accomplished player when I moved into the first XI the following year.

As for what might be labelled as 'coaching', at that stage I wasn't receiving any particularly significant technical input, but obviously Dad's guidance was important and just being around a number of people who had played a great deal of cricket, albeit at a relatively low level, was hugely influential. Even in the earliest years of county age group cricket, when teams tended to be run by teachers and other volunteers rather than by professional coaches, there was little technical tuition. That changed from when I was around 14 years of age when the likes of Nick Haynes and John Rowe became involved, and in his role as cricket development officer for Worcestershire, the former county opening batsman, Mark Scott, was in fairly regular attendance at junior county matches and training sessions. However, I would say that in those first few years, I was moving forward as a cricketer not as a result of any kind of structured development programme but through a somewhat random process of garnering information and experience from a wide variety of sources and in a range of contexts.

Away from cricket, I was growing up alongside my friends in very much the way they were. Life revolved around Bretforton Sports Club, known locally as 'the Bughut', and as well as cricket I have represented the village at football, darts, pool, dominoes, skittles and even cribbage! The club has remained my 'home from home' to this day and immediately upon my retirement from playing professional cricket, I welcomed the opportunity once again to play Sunday morning football for the village team which I had, of course, been unable to do for several years.

I have described the village as traditional, but I regard the Sports Club as unique. Its stalwarts comprise a very tight-knit community, based on a few families whose members have, in some cases for several generations, spent their leisure time making the club what it is – a vibrant social and sporting centre. When amongst those people I am truly myself and that will always be the case. I hope they regard me as the same character I have always been. The club takes great pride in my achievements for Worcestershire and I am hugely appreciative of the part it has played in making me who I am.

4

CUTTING IT

MY INVOLVEMENT with Worcestershire age group squads began at the Under-11 level. My first trial was at Perdiswell Leisure Centre in Worcester in late 1994 and I earned a place in the group as an all-rounder, batting at around No.6 and bowling a fair bit. At Under-12, though, I was given the opportunity to move up the order and I made a fifty in the first game away against Gloucestershire. At both Under-11 and Under-12, we had a pretty successful team and won an inter-counties festival in Cornwall in both those years.

Then, at the Under-13 stage, our coach, Les Bishop, introduced a policy whereby, unless match circumstances absolutely dictated otherwise, those who batted did not bowl and vice-versa. Not surprisingly, this did little for the prospects of several talented all-rounders in the group, and as a side we were less successful. I'm sure he meant well, and his intention was to prevent a few individuals from dominating what was, after all, a development project, but I am not convinced that it was an ideal philosophy. It didn't particularly damage my progress as I was much more concerned with batting than bowling, but for a lad like Craig Everett, a really talented cricketer who usually opened the bowling and batted at No.4, it was far from ideal. My first hundred for the county came at Under-13 level against Staffordshire at Walsall, and it was around that time that I felt I perhaps became the premier batsman in that age group and began to win what became a series of batting awards.

I continued to be a regular member of the county teams for the next few years, which involved a fair amount of driving for my parents since we practised and played at a variety of venues in both winter and summer. When the squads began to use the purpose-built cricket hall which had opened at Prince Henry's High School in Evesham at almost exactly the same time that I started there, their lives became a lot less complicated!

By the age of about 15, and once I had properly become part of the Worcestershire youth cricket programme, a more structured pattern was established. There were no academy teams at that point but there was a weekly classroom session at New Road, which covered topics such as fitness, nutrition and psychology and a net session each Sunday. The Easter holidays involved going to the ground on an almost daily basis as part of a pre-season programme and we would be required to bowl at the pros for an hour and a half or so each morning and afternoon before, if we were lucky, squeezing in a short session against the bowling machine at the end of the day. It was tough but, in many ways, a valuable introduction to the rigorous nature of professional cricket. I consider that to be the first stage of what was to become for me a hugely important player-coach relationship with Damian D'Oliveira.

My first outings as a second XI player came shortly afterwards, in 2002, whilst I was in my last year at school. On debut in a one-day game against Gloucestershire at Bristol, I didn't bat or bowl but then realised a long-held ambition by playing at New Road for the first time. Against quite a powerful Glamorgan bowling line-up I managed to hang around for about an hour and a half in scoring a scratchy 9 in the first innings, then managed 38 in the first innings against Leicestershire at Kidderminster at the end of the season. It wasn't exactly a blistering start but nor had I been out of my depth.

That winter, I applied for the club's scholarship place at the University of Worcester on what is now a well-established scheme which has seen a number of players successfully combine their studies with the first steps in a professional playing career, but my application was initially rejected. Damian D'Oliveira rang to say that the club was offering the place to a young seam bowler named Jonny Farrow who was coming down from Cheshire, but it was hoped that I would stick around and continue to play second XI cricket.

The situation changed within a few weeks when head coach, Tom Moody, instituted something of a cull among the playing staff which, alongside one or two retirements, freed up some money for another scholarship, thus allowing me to gain a place after all. I was to be paid £2,000 for the year but was not required to pay any tuition fees to the university. This proved to be an absolutely pivotal moment for me because I effectively became a professional cricketer.

I was still living at home so my student loan was spent on a Peugeot 106 and a routine of daily drives to Worcester began. As far as employing the playing staff, the club was still operating on a sixth-months basis in those days so participation in the winter programme was optional, involving a few Wednesday night trips to Edgbaston for indoor nets and three fitness sessions per week which, conveniently enough, took place at the university. But in the summer, both Jonny and I were treated the same as the rest of the staff. University commitments were fitted around our cricket and, as far as I was concerned, my professional career was underway.

In 2003, I scored almost 500 runs at an average of over 36 in the Second XI Championship and played a couple of particularly significant knocks. At Northampton, in a match we lost by an innings, I ground out 84 in five hours against an attack including a 23-year-old Monty Panesar, and then a couple of weeks later, I carried my bat for an unbeaten 143 out of a team total of 273 against Glamorgan at the beautiful Abergavenny ground.

I remember that Adrian Shaw was keeping wicket, and I was amused that his response when a bowler asked for a sweeper on the boundary was 'Bloody hell, he's not Brian Lara!' I couldn't argue, even though I was about 100 not out at the time! Again, I had occupied the crease for nearly five hours and I felt that not only was I making meaningful runs but I was growing up as a batsman and developing the mental and physical attributes required to play long innings. When we got back to Worcester after that game I remember Tom Moody congratulating me and even calling over the then Worcestershire chairman, John Elliott, to tell him I had carried my bat, which for him was especially praiseworthy. Such recognition is priceless for a young player and it remains in my mind as a very proud moment.

There was still a long way for me to go, however, before I ever felt remotely like I was going to break into the first team reckoning. In 2004, my second year of combining cricket and university studies, I continued to make progress but without managing anything particularly spectacular. A hundred in a Second XI Championship game against Glamorgan at Barnt Green was a decent enough effort and I averaged 36 in the second XI one-day competition which we won by beating an Essex side including Alastair Cook in the final. In most respects, though, it was a year of consolidation, of coming to terms with the requirements of professional sport, of observing the habits, good and bad, of others, of growing up and increasingly learning to take responsibility for my own development.

I recall some slight worries that the third year of my university scholarship might really be make or break; either I would get a proper contract or I'd be done and looking for a career outside the game. Then, the next season, things changed. It is always difficult to identify the specific factors which bring about an altered set of circumstances and perhaps they are just too variable and affected by too many elements to make such an assessment possible. As one player goes out of form, perhaps, another begins to prosper. An injury to a certain player might open up opportunities for an understudy. Anyway, for whatever reasons, 2005 was to be something of a watershed season for me.

Having made a fairly inauspicious first-class debut at Kidderminster in a defeat against the Loughborough University Centre of Cricketing Excellence (to give it its full name!), I was called up in somewhat unusual circumstances to play my first County Championship game against Somerset at Bath in early June. Gareth Batty was required to join the England squad at late notice after the start of the game and left at the end of the second day. He was batting towards the end of day two and decided that, as he was leaving that night, he would simply have a swing! He should have been out three or four times, pretty standard for Batts, but eventually reached the close unbeaten on 17. Had he been dismissed in that innings I would not have batted. As it turned out, I went to the crease in his place the following morning, and so I began my Championship career as what was termed an 'international replacement'. I lasted 25 balls before being lbw to Andrew Caddick for 4, although I like to claim a combined 21 for our No.7 slot! I wasn't required to bat in the second innings as Ben Smith and Stephen Moore saw us to an eight-wicket win.

It is amusing to consider the relative significance of a single event such as that debut in terms of its importance to the different parties involved. I doubt Gareth Batty really cared at that point who replaced him as he rushed off to join the England set-up. I suspect that Andrew Caddick does not especially count the 21-year-old Daryl Mitchell as a prized scalp amongst his 1,180 first-class wickets. And I rather think that Somerset's South African Test player, Graeme Smith, and his equally famous team-mate, the Sri Lankan, Sanath Jayasuriya, might have little recollection of my less than stunning entrance on to the Championship stage. For me, however, it was a big event and though I hadn't made much of an impact, I had enjoyed being around the first team and was keen for further opportunities.

The innings which probably did most to earn me my first proper professional contract came at Grace Road, Leicester just over a week later. Immediately after the game at Bath, Tom Moody left his position as Worcestershire head coach to take up a similar position with the Sri Lanka national side, and Steve Rhodes was placed in temporary charge of team matters. 'Bumpy' picked me to make a proper start in the side for the game against Leicestershire and though I was batting at No.6, I was well aware that I would need to have my wits about me as the opposition bowling attack included Ottis Gibson, Charl Willoughby, Claude Henderson and a very youthful Stuart Broad!

I went to the wicket fairly late on the second day to join Zander de Bruyn who was going well and I hung around till the close, managing a princely 3 not out of about 30 runs we added to that point. Now, I always think it is far too easy to overestimate the vagaries of fortune in cricket, those little slices of luck which change things dramatically, and I, perhaps even more than most professionals, preferred generally to take the view that you make your own luck through hard work, practice and determination. However, it is sometimes impossible to ignore the almost ridiculous, minuscule events which, when viewed through a different lens, could be seen to have shaped a career.

When I was caught in the gully early on off the bowling of Broad the fact that it was called a no-ball might at the time have seemed a minor detail to everybody concerned, including me. I was, of course, hugely relieved as is any batter who receives such a reprieve but no more than that. Subsequent events meant that Stuart's overstepping of the crease by a centimetre or two had a big impact on the rest of my life. I accept, of course, that it is perfectly possible that had I not made runs in that game at Grace Road, I would have done so somewhere else; had I not taken that opportunity others would have presented themselves and it could be foolish to exaggerate the significance of one moment. Yet it was the lifeline offered by that no-ball call which allowed me to go on to play a career-defining innings. I consider that term career-defining especially appropriate because the unbeaten 63 I managed took over five hours and 245 balls! I had gone in with the score on 129/4 and remained not out as we were dismissed for 323.

It felt almost like a rite of passage for me, partly, I think, because it began an inevitable toughening-up process which was to be an important next step. It was also the first time I had batted with Paul Nixon behind the stumps. Nicko, later to become a good mate, was never short of an opinion and this was my introduction to the 'friendly' chat in which he would inevitably attempt to engage a batsman. I also remember the experienced duo of Darren Maddy and John Sadler being moved to comment fairly regularly that they were less than impressed with the fluency of my strokeplay! Though we eventually lost a close one by 12 runs, two days later I was offered a full-time two-year professional contract. As a grateful beneficiary of the club's university scholarship scheme I had hitherto been treated like a young professional. Now, I was one.

I played three further Championship matches in that 2005 summer and passed 50 once more, against Essex at New Road, and I had begun to feel a little more composed in the first XI environment. I also played six Twenty20 games that campaign though my contributions were mainly with the ball. At that time, the Twenty20 competition was not taken as seriously as it was a few years later and it is indeed hard to equate those early games and their relatively relaxed nature with the tense, high-octane affairs in which I played in the later years of my career. Generally, whenever back in the second XI after my Championship debut, I was very confident and productive and finished the season at the top of the charts with over 700 runs at an average of 74.20. Those runs included 150 not out against Glamorgan (I was beginning to enjoy my encounters with them) plus 181 and 120 in the same game at Ombersley against a Warwickshire second XI which included Moeen Ali.

I was now mixing with, and playing alongside, those who a few years earlier had been my heroes as I watched cricket at New Road, and unsurprisingly, their example and advice was improving me as a player. Any Worcestershire junior cricketer in the 1990s was in awe of Graeme Hick whose performances for the county set new and, for me, unparalleled standards in what could be termed the modern era. At times it was hard to believe that I was playing and training alongside him. I vividly remember a pre-season intra-club practice match we had at Ombersley at the start of that season simply because it was the first time Hicky ever spoke to me, even though I can't really recall what he said! Vikram Solanki, the captain, was another wonderful player whom I had watched with wide-eyed admiration for a few years and for whom I had huge respect. Meanwhile, Ben Smith, or 'Uncle Ben' as Steve Davies and I used to call him, was a fount of knowledge and support when it came to batting.

It was also a rare privilege to share the dressing room with such huge characters as Chris Gayle and Chaminda Vaas. Chris was a particular favourite amongst us youngsters as he regularly spent time upstairs in the old junior dressing room, though his main reason for being there was usually to grab some sleep! In one game away against Yorkshire, I was performing 12th man duties, keenly trying to take everything in and to learn from the experience, and watched Chris open the batting with Stephen Moore.

It was Headingley in September and not surprisingly, at the start of the game, the South African seamer, Deon Kruis, was a handful. I was fascinated to watch Gayle's approach as he simply threw the bat at virtually every ball before being caught at third man for 29 off 17 balls having hit seven fours. I plucked up the courage to ask about his mindset. 'Well,' he said, 'I played and missed at the first ball I faced and it seamed so much that I just decided that I might as well make runs while I could before I got another one like that!' And that was it! It was just amazing to hear a top player describe the game in such simple terms and, though his process was about as far removed from mine as it was possible to imagine, I was oddly impressed. I think that was actually the last game of County Championship cricket that Chris ever played but his stellar career across the globe in all formats for the next 20 years or so shows that it is not necessary to over-complicate things in order to be successful.

As my university course had ended, I was ready to focus fully on cricket and the obvious thing to do was to attempt to play for 12 months of the year. After most county clubs went full-time, this was no longer an issue for young players but up to that point many, like me, turned their attention to the southern hemisphere. Even in the era of year-round training some up-and-coming county players still travel overseas in the winter to broaden their horizons with some club or grade cricket, but for two or three decades it was very much the norm.

Every October, airports in Auckland, Sydney, Melbourne, Perth and Johannesburg would welcome a variety of young British lads, often travelling abroad alone for the first time, wide-eyed, wet behind the ears and overflowing with enthusiasm. Usually, they came back better, tougher cricketers and often more mature, independent people who had learned a lot of lessons, not necessarily all related to the game! Many travelled abroad for the winter straight from school and though that worked for some, I am convinced that the way it fell out for me was more suited to my character. I felt that if I abandoned my education immediately after the sixth form, intending to return to it after a gap year spent playing cricket in some far-flung country, that proposed reunion might never take place, and I also believe that at 21 years of age I was better placed to make the most of such an experience than I would have been three years earlier.

Midland Guildford in Perth, Western Australia was to be my destination for the 2005/06 English winter, the first of three successive seasons that I spent with them. I was treading a fairly well-worn path as Worcestershire players who had previously played for the club included Vikram Solanki, Stephen Moore, Chris Liptrot and Kabir Ali, most of those placements facilitated via Tom Moody, of course, whose hometown club it was. Other famous Australian players to have played there are Brendon Julian, Simon Katich, Bruce Yardley and Tim Zoehrer, and I know Alec Stewart regards the eight successive years he spent with the club to be a vital part of his development.

It was the first time I had ever been abroad alone but I felt excited at the prospect rather than nervous, genuinely believing that it was coming at just the right time for me. On arrival in Perth, I was immediately introduced to what became my surrogate family, Tom and Bridget Pivac, their daughters and son, Chris, who played at the club. They were a tremendous support to me during my time there and it was the start of an enduring friendship.

Eventually, I shared accommodation with one of the other players, Peter Worthington, who was a part of the Western Australia (WA) squad at the time. My Sunday trips to the Pivac household for a proper feed were a welcome relief from a fairly chaotic but thoroughly enjoyable home life! There was perhaps only one time throughout the whole three trips I made to Australia that I felt a little homesick and that was when, after the first week of being spoiled at the Pivacs, I moved into the flat, before Pete's arrival, and sat on a bean bag, next to a mattress on the floor, eating a cheese sandwich for my tea and watching a small, portable television which boasted four channels I didn't recognise!

Once the cricket got underway, I was in my element. After a couple of training sessions, I began in the club's second grade XI and though I didn't make many runs in the first few games, I then made a 99 and a double hundred to force my way into the senior side. Even in the early games at the lower level, I was contributing with the ball and quietly confident that when I eventually made it into the first grade, I would be able to handle it.

The cricket at that higher grade was tough, especially if WA did not have a game that weekend because the first-class players would then be involved. Against Melville, their attack included Chris Tremlett as an overseas player, his fellow Hampshire player, Dimi Mascarenhas, whose home club it was, Steve Magoffin, who, of course, would later play for the Pears, and a fellow called Duncan Spencer, who, it's fair to say, had a somewhat tumultuous injury-plagued career but, believe me, he bowled a quick ball!

The pitches were generally excellent, being fast and bouncy, which encouraged pace bowlers, but also suited my game which at that stage (some would argue for the next 15 years as well) was still based mainly on blocking, steering and deflecting the ball, rather than striking it in front of the wicket. I certainly developed my back foot play significantly on those surfaces, becoming much more proficient at playing the cut shot and improving my pulling of the short ball. I became fitter, too, as in that first year, the Worcestershire Supporters' Association provided some funding for a personal trainer, with whom I followed a programme of early morning workouts, and very generously a small amount of pocket money.

I undoubtedly thrived in the fierce playing environment, and thoroughly enjoyed the twice weekly club training sessions followed by a few beers with the boys in the clubroom, alongside the unbelievably competitive cut and thrust on the field.

There was very much a no-holds-barred, almost stereotypically Australian, attitude in the middle and I was regularly reminded of my Pommie status, but within five minutes of walking off the field would be happily sharing a drink with opponents and team-mates alike.

I was never particularly bothered by the heat and was perhaps a little casual about sun protection as at one stage I developed a small but benign melanoma on my face. It came to nothing but taught me another important lesson. On my subsequent visits to Perth, I was provided with better accommodation, a job in a sports shop and decent transport, but in that first year I had pretty basic digs and a succession of unreliable vehicles which frequently broke down. All of this ensured that I grew up as a young man, learning to organise my time and fend for myself in terms of cooking, cleaning, laundry and other such mundane but important matters.

I returned to England ready for the start of the 2006 season a better prepared, more rounded and more mature individual than previously. My game was in decent shape, I was fit and strong, and I had a two-year contract. It was time to find out if I had what it took to make a meaningful career in the game.

5

UPSTAIRS, DOWNSTAIRS

IF THERE was a spate of absenteeism suffered by several employers in the Vale of Evesham on the morning of 3 August 2006 they might have been able to discover the reason had they been keen followers of county cricket. A fairly large contingent of my close friends at Bretforton Sports Club took the day off work and made an early morning start heading to Colwyn Bay in north Wales having heard that I was 87 not out at the end of the first day's play in Worcestershire's away game against Glamorgan. They were keen to be there if I were to make a maiden first-class century.

I had started the season in the Championship team and played in the first two games, against Somerset and Derbyshire, which were both home defeats. I was opening the batting and in those four knocks managed a fifty in the first innings against Somerset, but otherwise performed modestly. After that I was included in most games in the Twenty20 though my only real contributions were with the ball, but I had continued to score pretty heavily in second XI cricket and made a couple of big hundreds, 141 at Old Hill against Glamorgan (who else?) and 158 away against Surrey. So, when Graeme Hick suffered a hand injury against Derbyshire at Chesterfield, I earned a recall for the game against the Welshmen at Colwyn Bay and was to bat at No.6.

Our skipper, Vikram Solanki, won the toss and decided to bat and though we lost a couple of wickets fairly early on, a decent third-wicket partnership of 61 between him and Ben Smith meant that at one stage we were 107/2. However, with Vikram and Steve Davies both dismissed in early afternoon the score was 147/4 when I went in and Ben was out almost immediately after I had joined him. On the small, fairly quick-scoring ground I shared a good stand with Gareth Batty of 75 before being joined by Roger Sillence who struck a run-a-ball 63, which included six fours and four sixes. Zaheer Khan and Matt Mason also played useful cameos before being dismissed and when the ninth wicket fell the score had reached 377/9, which remained the overnight position.

As I walked out to bat on the second morning the sight of Paul Jones, who is about 6ft 9in and one of my best mates from home, peering over the wall at the side of the ground as he waited to gain access made me smile. I was aware of the opportunity on offer, and also that a good number of Bret lads had made the trip, which I guess added a bit of pressure. But I was reasonably calm and confident that I could manage the 13 runs I needed, provided, of course, that my partner, last man Nadeem Malik, could survive as well. That proved not to be an issue as he went on to record the third-highest score of his career before being out lbw to Robert Croft for 35 with the total on 460 after we had added 83 for the last wicket.

I am told that the roar that greeted my hundred would have suggested to an outsider that it was actually a home batter who had passed a milestone, and especially observant students of accent might have noted something of an Evesham (or 'Asum' as the locals say) twang in amongst the congratulatory shouts! I finished unbeaten on 134 and we went on to win the game by 311 runs, which in those days for a Pears side without Graeme Hick was quite something. It's fair to say that I returned a slightly different young man. Having made a big score, I genuinely felt that I belonged at first XI level.

With Hicky still not having recovered from his hand injury, the team was unchanged for the next match at home against Surrey and though we were hammered in an innings defeat, I played what to this day I regard as one of my best ever knocks in compiling an unbeaten 54 in our first innings of 304, against an attack dominated by the spin duo of Anil Kumble and Ian Salisbury, who took nine of the ten wickets to fall. Despite that effort, I was quickly treated to a demonstration of just how harsh professional cricket can be, when Steve Rhodes took the decision to leave me out for the following game at Leicester owing to Graeme's return. It was a tough call to take and one of which I frequently reminded Bumpy in the years ahead!

Two wins in the last two Championship games ensured that the county gained promotion to Division One, the outcome eventually sealed when a victory at Northampton on the last day coincided with an Essex defeat at Leicester. Not being involved, I was watching a 2-0 win over Charlton Athletic at Villa Park when the news came through. With promotion in the Pro40 League having been secured a week earlier, the season ended on a high and there was much to look forward to in 2007. I had finished with an average of 47 in first-class cricket and was content enough with my progress.

Another turning point in my life occurred late in that summer of 2006, though it's fair to say that I wasn't aware at the time quite how significant it would be. On one of my fairly routine nights out with my mates, we made a customary visit to Evesham's only real nightspot, *Marilyn's*, and there I was introduced to a young local girl named Danni. One of her friends told her that I had been on Sky TV and, knowing little or nothing about cricket, she naturally presumed I was some sort of presenter. I suppose I must have impressed her, and soon we established that shortly we were both bound for Australia; me to play another season in Perth and Danni to travel. We agreed to get together on the Gold Coast. Our phone calls between Perth and Sydney became increasingly frequent and once we eventually did meet up again she abandoned her travels and we have remained together ever since!

Back at New Road for the start of the 2007 season, following another tough but successful campaign with Midland Guildford, this time playing first grade cricket the whole time, I was delighted, along with Steve Davies, whom I had played alongside since my youth cricket days, to receive recognition as a senior player. For both of us, this came not with any cap or salary increase but an invitation to move downstairs from the junior dressing room to the senior changing area. To those who never experienced the old-fashioned segregation in existence at many county clubs in the past, this might seem fairly mundane, but to us it was very important.

It was another rite of passage, this time a literal one, a clear indication of our recognised status in the team hierarchy.

We were joined in our new-found corner of the downstairs dressing room by a newcomer who was to become one of my closest friends in the game for the remainder of my career in Moeen Ali, who had made the move down the M5 from Edgbaston. Mo and I knew each other quite well having played against each other on more than a few occasions in youth, second XI and club cricket, but, of course, neither of us knew at that point how closely intertwined our lives and careers were to become.

What followed in that flood-ravaged summer was ultimately a period of frustration for me as a player. I was thrilled to properly be a part of a group which included several big characters and to mix daily with them. The captain, Vikram Solanki, had always been a hugely impressive personality for me and his authority and moral compass have left an indelible impression, whilst I attempted to learn as much as possible from the other senior figures by whom I was surrounded. Gareth Batty's sense of fun, Hicky's matchless example in terms of preparation, diet, training and focus, and Ben Smith's guidance on batting, were all influential as were other senior guys like Ray Price, Phil Jacques and Stephen Moore. However, my opportunities at first XI level were limited. I played in a pre-season friendly against Somerset at Taunton and made a hundred in an early first-class game against Loughborough UCCE at Worcester but after that, until August, I was mainly restricted to a diet of Birmingham League cricket for Halesowen, and second XI stuff despite a few outings in Twenty20 games.

All of that season's travails have to be set against the background of absolute turmoil caused by the almost unprecedented summer floods which caused unimaginable disruption that year. On 25 June, the New Road ground suffered its first summer flood since 1969 and the tenth-worst of the 135 such events since 1899. Three weeks later, on 16 July, thanks to the efforts of club staff supplemented by an army of volunteers, the ground was passed fit for the Championship match against Lancashire to begin on the 19th. Then, on the morning the game was due to start, the rains returned, and two days later the ground was submerged again, this time to the second-highest depth ever recorded.

No more cricket would be played at New Road that season. We had no training facilities and were forced to play home games at a variety of borrowed venues, to practise when and wherever we could and generally, to get by via whatever means possible. Financially, Worcestershire CCC was pushed to the brink and as players we were, like all the club's employees, simply battling to survive.

One particular personal memory stands out. Amidst the devastation, I made a trip to the ground in an attempt to rescue my own kit from the submerged dressing room, part of me wishing that I was still based upstairs! I climbed down a ladder from one of the hospitality areas in the old executive suite, put on a pair of waders and plunged into the murky waters inside. As I was retrieving my belongings from a fortunately situated overhead locker, I noticed a long cardboard box floating by which had my name on it. It contained a new bat from my sponsor. Having fished it from the waters, I took it home and saw that it had sustained only minor damage and looked in reasonable order apart from a smallish stain on the back of the blade. It seemed a tad heavy, having perhaps soaked up a little moisture, but was otherwise intact so I deposited it in my airing cupboard for a few months and the following season it turned out to be one of the best bats I ever had!

The reason for my frustration in that disjointed season can, I suppose, be put down to the fact that though I was very much the next batsman in line for opportunities at first team level, the injuries or loss of form which could have opened the door for me simply never came. In one-day cricket, it was often a straight choice between Moeen and myself for a place in the side and though I played some part in all forms of the game I only occasionally felt that I was truly an integral member of the team. I managed only four Championship appearances with a highest score of 70 not out when carrying my bat in an innings defeat against

Sussex at Hove, though remarkably, I did finish at the top of both the first-class batting and bowling averages for the club thanks to my early season runs against the Loughborough students and my five fairly inconsequential Championship wickets at 21.80 each.

Despite only one four-day win and relegation from Division One in the Championship we did qualify for the quarter-final of the Twenty20 competition after finishing third in the Midlands/Wales/West group but lost to Gloucestershire in a rain-reduced game at Bristol. That was one of only three appearances I made in that format where I was still very much being included for my bowling, and I did not feature at all in the 50-over competition.

Nonetheless, I had maintained decent enough form in second XI cricket and was delighted to play more than a bit part role in what was a successful campaign in the club's NatWest Pro40 League title win. For Worcestershire to have ended what was in so many ways a catastrophic season with some silverware was absolutely remarkable and though it might seem unlikely given my personal frustrations, I was hugely honoured to have contributed. I made five appearances and was in the side that sealed the title in front of the TV cameras under the lights at Bristol.

My two close friends, Moeen and Steve Davies, shared a magnificent opening stand of 151 in under 17 overs as we chased down a target of 271 to win with 11 balls to spare and it was a memorable evening. The club's first title in 13 years, coming as it did at the end of months of turmoil, was a proud achievement and given that we had hardly been able to practise properly for that or any other variety of the game, all the more praiseworthy. It remains a highlight when I reflect on my career and when future generations look down the list of the club's honours it will stand comparison with any.

At the end of the season I attended the PCA Awards dinner at the Albert Hall hoping not to embarrass myself as I had two years previously. Then, as a raw youth and having perhaps had a drink too many, I got my aim slightly wrong in the gents and managed to spray the smart shoes of the gentleman standing beside me. As I muttered a garbled apology, I noticed that it was an unimpressed John Major!

On this occasion I was sitting next to Hicky, and as we looked at the auction items I mentioned that several of them looked attractive. In response to my suggestion that he must have dozens of items of memorabilia, Graeme assured me that he didn't really go in for that kind of thing and only kept a few pieces of particular significance to him. 'But if you fancy something why don't you put in the minimum bid?' he said. 'You might be lucky and get one of them.' I have no doubt now that he saw me as a wide-eyed youth somewhat awestruck by the occasion. He knew he was stitching me up.

I won all three of the items I bid for: a picture of Pelé with Muhammad Ali, a signed 1966 World Cup photo montage and a signed Martin Johnson Rugby World Cup picture and left £1,450 worse off. Try explaining that to your partner when you're saving for a deposit on your first house!

In his summary of the 2007 season in the Worcestershire yearbook, the renowned cricket journalist, George Dobell, then with the *Birmingham Post*, wrote that I was 'A resolute batsman and nerveless limited overs bowler' who would 'soon command a place in both forms of the game.' He added: 'Sure, there are plenty of more attractive, more flash cricketers around but few have the character and resilience of Mitchell. Expect him to open in the Championship of 2008.' George was right and the following season I became central to the county's on-field strategy in all cricket.

6

YO-YO YEARS (1)

FOOTBALL CLUBS which tend to oscillate between the Premier League and the Championship in England, too good for the second tier but perhaps not up to the standard required to maintain top flight status, tend to be labelled 'yo-yo clubs'. Much the same might be said about the Worcestershire cricket sides of my era. In ten of the first 14 seasons in which I played first XI cricket, we were either promoted or relegated in the County Championship and it was a recurring pattern only broken when the coronavirus pandemic forced a restructuring of the competition in my final two seasons. Whilst on the one hand ensuring that there was nearly always something to play for in red-ball cricket, nobody associated with the club would claim that it was a desirable state of affairs; the aim was always to achieve then maintain a place at the top table.

Our elevation to Division One at the conclusion of the 2008 season offered what I thought was, certainly in my career to that point, our best chance to stay up. We had enjoyed a very solid campaign in the longer format, winning six and only losing two of our 16 games. Former Ashes hero, Simon Jones, was recruited from Glamorgan to form a superb dual spearhead to our attack with Kabir Ali, the pair taking over 100 wickets between them, and they were well supported by the rest of the bowlers, including another new boy, Gareth Andrew, who had joined from Somerset. With Stephen Moore, Vikram Solanki and Ben Smith all passing 1,000 runs and Graeme Hick, in his final season, still averaging 45.93, scoring runs had not been a problem and I, too, had played my part.

A third English winter spent in the Australian sunshine, this time with Danni alongside me, had offered me the chance to gain some valuable captaincy know-how. Leading Midland Guildford in the first grade was an honour and a challenge I very much enjoyed. As well as the tactical, on-field awareness that I developed, it was my initial experience of involvement in team selection, strategic planning and handling interpersonal relationships from a leadership angle. All of which I found interesting, challenging and rewarding. Having to satisfactorily explain to a player why he has been omitted from the team or perhaps moved in the batting order might seem routine parts of the job but they are facets which you need to learn to approach correctly if you are to become a good captain. So once again, I felt that on my return home I had grown as a cricketer in more than one regard.

I played, and opened the batting, in every Championship game that 2008 season, scoring 856 runs at an average of 38.90 with one hundred, against Essex at Colchester, and three fifties. It was my consistency, though, which pleased me the most and which probably helped me cement that spot at the top of the order. I found the first of several trusty opening partners in my career in Stephen Moore, who that year was in the form of his life, and we added over 100 for the first wicket on five occasions, three of which came in the space of four innings in consecutive matches against Glamorgan at New Road and Middlesex at Lord's. As with other batting buddies with whom I would have similar purple patches in future years, it is not easy to pinpoint the factors that made it work. Stephen was a quiet character but very focused and supportive in the middle, where his tempo generally matched my own. I enjoyed his company, we generally ran well and I learned a lot from his measured approach. That year, Stephen was the first batsman in the country to pass 1,000 runs and finished as top first-class run-scorer with 1,451.

Also, in keeping with the Dobell prediction, I became a regular in List A cricket, too, and recorded a 50-over career-best 92 away against Somerset. Another notable achievement was recording the best Twenty20 bowling figures ever for the county when I bagged 4-11 against Gloucestershire. Though we hadn't progressed to the later stages of either the 50-over competition or the Twenty20 Cup, we had maintained our status in the top tier of the Pro40 competition. Being recognised as the fans' Fielder of the Year and given the 'Moment of the Year' award for hitting a boundary off the last ball to secure a tie in a televised Pro40 game, also at Taunton, were minor accolades but further evidence that I was becoming, like my sofa ten years later, part of the furniture.

So why didn't that talented squad, certainly the best I had ever played in up to that point, and arguably one of the most capable of which I was ever a member, manage to maintain a spot in Division One in 2009? Well, first and foremost, Graeme Hick retired at the end of 2008. Even though his mighty powers were slightly on the wane as he entered his forties, he was to the end a colossal presence in any Worcestershire XI. Though there are many figures in the county's history who deserve the label of 'Mr Worcestershire' coined by that Middlesex commentator with reference to myself, it is difficult to look beyond Graeme.

His figures are breathtaking – 65 Test matches for England plus 120 ODIs, 526 first-class games (384 for Worcestershire), 136 first-class centuries (106 for Worcestershire!) and 232 first-class wickets (185 for Worcestershire). A top score of 405 not out is almost unimaginable for most of us, as is scoring 1,000 runs by the end of May, as Graeme did in 1988. Add in 651 List A career appearances and another 22,000 runs, the bulk of which were for the Pears, and the likes of myself start to pale, if not quite into insignificance, then close to it! Oh, and by the way, he also took 528 catches for the county in first-class cricket. My 295 puts me a very proud eighth in the all-time list but Graeme is way out in front and a huge 113 ahead of Dick Richardson in second place. Remarkably, the pair played almost exactly the same number of games for the county; Hick 384 and Richardson 383.

Removing a player like that from a team is bound to have an effect but I sometimes wonder if it was not the lack of his contributions on the scorecard which was most damaging but simply his absence from the whole setup. How can you calculate such things? I cannot say that there was anything specific which Graeme took with him nor that his presence alone ever guaranteed success, but his example, in so many ways, was crucial. And if it had inspired and taught me, then it must have had a similar effect on others. The way in which one member of a dressing room can influence those around him or her, is surely one of the most interesting and unfathomable aspects of a team dynamic. Just as a 'bad apple' can poison a group, so a good one can have an opposite impact and that, I guess, is the way it has always been and always will be, regardless of advances in coaching, analysis or tactical awareness.

My own memories of Hicky are two-fold. From the first time I met him, having as a schoolboy marvelled from the boundary at his prowess, he was never anything other than exemplary in terms of his off-field behaviour. He was quiet, polite, thoughtful and considerate, able to take a joke and to give a bit of gentle stick but never overstepped the mark – an ideal dressing room member. At the beginning, I found it hard to pick his brains for helpful information but later he became a brilliant source of ideas. I can't say I blame him for that early reticence as by the time I came along he'd probably already had 20 years of young wannabes pestering him!

He practised assiduously and always with a purpose, never falling into the trap that many players do, of losing concentration towards the end of a net or a session of throw-downs and messing around a little, having a slog or trying a few experimental shots. He attempted to hit every ball with absolute precision, for a spell favouring practice with a 'half bat', a specially cut-down, narrow blade, and still, it seemed to me, hitting almost everything in the middle. His hunger for runs in such a long career was simply amazing and I cannot think of another cricketer with whom I played who comes close in that regard.

When it came to the physical aspect of training, Hicky was what we called a machine and at 40 was still up with the best of us in the fitness tests. In the dining room or the bar, however, he was able to curb his appetite with tremendous control; I noticed very early on that he always ate the right food and the right amount at the right time. Graeme was the ultimate professional and though blessed with huge natural talent, he did everything within his power to maximise it. I like to think I took a great deal from that; if somebody with so much more ability than me applied themselves in such a conscientious way then I realised early on that if I wanted to do well I needed to take note.

The other side of the man was only revealed on the field. There Hicky was masterful. I have to this day never seen anybody time the ball better. The way that he could force spinners off the back foot and still beat the sweeper on the cover boundary was always a marvel to me, but overall what I recall is the way he kept things so simple, and for that reason I was somewhat surprised when he went into coaching. To him, if the bowler pitched the ball up, you just smashed it back over his head and he couldn't understand why everybody else didn't just do the same!

One particular recollection I have is of a Pro40 game in 2007 at Trent Bridge when I was still relatively raw, especially in the shorter formats. I batted at No.7 and joined him with the score on 136/5 as we attempted to post a meaningful target. There must have been about ten overs remaining in the innings and Graeme Swann was in the middle of a fairly miserly spell. 'How do you want to play it?' I asked Hicky. His reply of, 'Well you just get yourself in,' was less precise than I might have expected but helped to settle my nerves. He was just so confident in his own ability to manage the situation that I felt less pressure than I might have had he given me instructions to get him on strike or reach a certain score by a specific over.

A few minutes later, I asked if I should try to get off strike to give him more opportunity to attack the bowling and he said, 'Yes if you like but just play it as you see it.' With three or four overs remaining, I asked if he thought I should take a punt and try to find the ropes or if there were any particular areas of the field we ought to be targeting and he said, 'Well if it's there just hit it!' Anyway, I must have done okay because I finished on 34 not out off 28 balls, he was unbeaten on 93 off 81 balls and our total of 225/5 was enough to win the game.

What struck me most at the time was just how relaxed and straightforward his approach was. There is no doubt in my mind that too many players and coaches overcomplicate the game and though Graeme's advice to me that day might sound unhelpful, it was far from it. It allowed me to feel less pressure than might otherwise have been the case and came, I'm certain, from his own sense of responsibility for the management of the situation. I also learned a massive amount from him about slip catching. He was, as his record suggests, just a genius in the cordon. Mostly, he would stand at second slip, a position I later made my own, and the spot where, I believe, most catches are taken off the quicker bowlers. When I stood slightly wider at third slip, there was an unspoken understanding that anything on the inside, meaning between me and him, was basically to be ignored! No surprise, then, that Graham Gooch once went on record as saying that his ideal slip cordon would be the Australian, Mark Taylor, Ian Botham and Hicky.

The passing of a true legend, then, was one factor in the team's underachievement in 2009 but, as I have previously suggested, it does not really explain what was a dismal season. Yet at the start, it seemed that everything was in place for us to go well. We had switched, for the first time ever, to 12-month contracts and had a fairly successful pre-season tour to Potchefstroom in South Africa where we came up against a 16-year-old left-handed wicketkeeper-batsman called Quinton de Kock, who liked to smash the ball to all parts. Potchefstroom itself was quiet, and with little to do the tour was appropriately cricket focused, one outstanding memory being when we played a game in the grounds of a psychiatric hospital. One of the pavilion attendants who was a genuinely lovely, helpful presence all day, was afflicted with a personality disorder and was convinced that he was Elvis Presley! Remember what I said about how cricket has helped me to learn about so many aspects of life which I would never otherwise have encountered!

So, we went into that year full of positive expectation. The New Road ground was back to its splendid best and the new Graeme Hick pavilion would open in May, providing superb facilities for the players. We had a serious belief that with that team we could realistically compete in Division One of the County Championship. Stephen Moore had enjoyed a successful England Lions tour over the winter in New Zealand and Moeen was beginning to look like the all-round star he would become.

In fact, the wheels came off almost from the outset. Simon Jones did not bowl a single ball following knee surgery and Kabir Ali played only four Championship games owing to hamstring and back injuries. The seam attack, so potent the year before, relied too heavily upon the aging

Matt Mason who, by then, was also the bowling coach, despite the early promise of youngsters like Richard Jones and Chris Whelan. Another factor was the disappointing performance, with the ball at least, of Ashley Noffke, our Australian overseas player.

We needed the batsmen to step up but managed only 30 batting bonus points all season – the lowest tally in the division. I was the only one to pass 1,000 Championship runs and in all honesty, that owed almost everything to what was to remain a career-best score of 298 in the penultimate game at Taunton. People often suggest to me that this was my finest ever effort with the bat and while numerically that might be the case, I don't consider it as such. The pitch was flat and the result a dull draw. One quirky statistic I later learned was that I had actually become the first player in the entire history of first-class cricket to be dismissed for 298!

We became the first Worcestershire side not to win a Championship game since 1928 and our relegation had already been confirmed before the trip to Taunton. Even though we won more one-day matches than we lost in 2009, we succumbed in three vital 'must win' games, failed to qualify for the later rounds of either of the two knockout competitions and finished third in the Pro40 League, the only format in which we played any consistently good cricket. In the 50-over competition a heavy defeat at home to Ireland when we managed to be dismissed for 58, Worcestershire's lowest ever List A total, was especially disappointing and taken as a whole it was a chastening year. Personally, I had averaged 38.73 in four-day cricket, had career bests with bat and ball (4-49 against Yorkshire at Headingley) and, having moved into the second slip berth, again won the fans' fielding award. In the previous summer I had bought my first house in the city and was playing regularly in all formats, but although my own mind and game were in reasonable shape, there wasn't a huge amount to celebrate.

My personal situation might have been pretty settled but that was clearly not the case for several of my team-mates and the end of that grim season marked something of a changing of the guard. Stephen Moore believed that his ambition to play Test cricket would be better served by playing in the top division, and left for Lancashire. Having spent countless hours alongside him at slip I knew that Steve Davies, who harboured realistic hopes of further international honours and had, with Gareth Batty, played for England in the 2009 Twenty20 series against West Indies, had agonised for some time over his future and whether ambition outweighed loyalty. In the end, both left for Surrey and were huge losses. Batts had generally been a lively, motivational presence whilst Davo was obviously one of our most talented emerging stars.

I did not disapprove of these moves. They, like me, had chosen a career which is generally short and precarious. Any cricketer who, in all good faith, does what he thinks is best in terms of improving his prospects does not deserve judgement from those around him or her. Simon Jones left for Hampshire where he was joined, after a fall-out with the club which involved him absenting himself from winter training, by Kabir Ali. I was aware that Batts had not always seen eye-to-eye with our coach, Steve ('Bumpy') Rhodes, and there had been gripes from senior players about the club's lack of ambition and our poor practice and injury rehabilitation facilities, but I don't think any of us were really prepared for such an exodus. Concern was expressed amongst the Worcestershire membership and there were even some calls for Bumpy to be replaced as director of cricket.

Against such a worrying backdrop there had been some important new additions to the playing staff, however, several of whom would actually go on to be serious contributors to the cause over the coming seasons. Wicketkeeper Ben Cox had made his debut in 2009, as had left-arm seam bowler, Jack Shantry, and in the winter we were joined by Alan Richardson. Richo was already in his mid-30s, having played previously for Derbyshire, Warwickshire and Middlesex, and it is fair to say that his signing was not widely regarded as a masterstroke. In fact, he was to become the absolute lynchpin of our seam attack for the next four seasons and for him to become one of Wisden's five Cricketers of the Year for 2011, at the age of 36, was a magnificent achievement.

Playing for any other county had at that stage never been a consideration for me and my appointment as Vikram Solanki's vice-captain for the 2010 season was a great honour and further strengthened my commitment to the Pears. I have already mentioned the enormous regard I had for Vikram as a cricketer and a person. Whereas Hicky might have been the most powerful batsman with whom I had ever shared a partnership, Vikram was comfortably the most elegant, and his cover drive was the stuff of dreams. He was always a player I would take the time to watch if I was not actually in the middle with him. To be asked to be his deputy was an accolade which meant a lot to me and I looked forward to playing a more active role in shaping team strategy on and off the field, though with Bumpy in overall charge you could never expect to be too influential!

The Australian opener Phil Jacques, who had played well for us in two brief spells in 2006 and 2007, had rejoined, and together we made a good start to the Championship season by sharing a century first-wicket partnership in the opening win over Middlesex at New Road. It was the first time the county had won its opening game in the competition since 2005 and, given that there had been precisely zero victories the season before, quite a psychological milestone. Poor old Steven Finn returned match figures of 14-106 and still finished on the losing side! My own first innings 85 was comfortably the highest individual score of a pretty low-scoring game and marked the beginning of the best season of my career to that point.

Unusually we had a ten-day break after that game and Jacquesy took the opportunity to enjoy a short break with his pregnant wife, Jess, in Tenerife, intending to return in plenty of time for our next fixture against Surrey at Whitgift School. Unfortunately for them the Icelandic volcano Eyjafjallajokull chose that week to erupt and the resulting ash cloud seriously disrupted air travel. Desperate to get back, Phil managed to get to mainland Spain where he hired a car before embarking upon a 48-hour drive through Spain and France to catch a ferry to Dover. The journey was punctuated by frequent stops for Jess, who was suffering from morning sickness. Eventually he made it to Whitgift only to bag a pair!

Thereafter, though, our form, like the weather, was somewhat patchy but by the halfway point we were third in Division Two, having taken the most batting bonus points of any team. Inconsistency, however, was the trademark of our four-day cricket alongside what was frankly very ordinary form in the one-day stuff. We lost the first seven games in the ECB's new 40-over competition (which had basically replaced the old Pro40 League and the 50-over knockout) and suffered six consecutive defeats in the Twenty20 Cup to finish bottom of our group.

At the beginning of August, and with our focus firmly back on the longer game after spending most of the previous two months losing one-day matches of one form or another, I hit a hot streak, recording three hundreds in consecutive knocks. At Cheltenham, I followed up a first-innings 104 with an unbeaten 134 as we chased down 339 to win a contest in which Gloucestershire had made 480 in their first dig! I think their skipper, Alex Gidman, who would, of course, later become a key figure at New Road, might have regretted his decision not to enforce the follow-on! Then in the next game, against Glamorgan at Colwyn Bay, where I hadn't played since that memorable occasion four years earlier, I managed another big not out score, 165, though this time in a losing cause. Despite some obvious personal satisfaction there was little to celebrate, though, as at the conclusion of the game our captain resigned and, in a hastily arranged conversation outside the changing room, Bumpy asked me if I would take over for the remainder of the season. It was a bombshell moment for us all, I think.

Vikram had been captain since 2005 and for almost every player in that team, with the possible exception of

Matt Mason, the only Pears skipper they had known. He had become chair of the PCA in 2009 and it must have been difficult to balance the demands of that role with those of captaincy. Little did I know at that point that I would also, one day in the not-too-distant future, learn first-hand the responsibilities of that very position. Additionally, our inconsistent form was clearly weighing heavily upon him and he felt the time was right for change.

It was an emotional dressing room to which Vik announced his decision and there were certainly a few tears. In the apparently tough, cut-throat world of professional sport, there is still, believe me, a lot of sentiment when it comes to interpersonal relationships, and the collective respect for our outgoing leader was enormous. He was, and remains, a figure of calm authority, intelligent, articulate and universally respected. He was not a captain who would regularly and angrily berate the side after a disappointing performance, although he had his moments, but his usually fairly brief addresses to the troops, whether before, during or after a session or a day's play, were generally delivered with such clarity and purpose that everybody in the room inevitably paid attention. None of us had seen his decision coming and, for me, there was no sense of achievement or pride at that time, the mood certainly being one of collective despondency.

I very briefly led the side in a washed-out game against the Pakistan tourists that lasted only 28 overs before the next Championship encounter against Surrey at New Road. This turned out to be a superb win by 238 runs, with Shakib Al Hasan taking eight wickets in the match and helping to propel us to fourth in the table with three games remaining.

It was also memorable for another reason as there was an extraordinary incident on the last day involving the returning Gareth Batty. As we skittled them in the second innings Batts was the fourth man out in a remarkable collapse which saw Surrey lose their last six wickets for 18 runs. As he left the field he became involved in a verbal altercation with a home supporter who was perhaps questioning the wisdom of his decision to quit the Pears the previous winter.

The spat continued when he reappeared on the pavilion balcony before he went and sat next to a spectator in the members' area. Ian Salisbury, one of the Surrey coaches, eventually intervened and calm was restored but seeing a player engage so vehemently with an abusive spectator was certainly a first for me. Though we found it amusing as we watched from the middle, and Batts may well be one of the more fiery characters in the game, it was still a clear reminder that those cat-calls from the crowd do hurt. The lasting memory I have of the incident is actually tinged with sadness. I have always believed that Worcestershire is a genuinely welcoming club and it was painful to see a friend who had previously served it with great distinction so upset.

A draw in a rain-affected game at Northampton was followed by a brilliant win over Middlesex at Lord's when Shakib took a remarkable 7-32 in 11.1 overs as we bowled them out for 66 in just over 31 overs!

An orthodox slow left-arm spinner, who had joined us in July at the conclusion of Bangladesh's two-Test series with England, Shakib's 35 wickets in eight games gave us a welcome boost as we suddenly found ourselves in with an outside chance of promotion. I felt that I was growing into the captaincy and as well as helping to reignite our interest in promotion I had presided over a series of good results in the 40-over competition since being given the reins. In one of those wins, at The Oval, we had made 376/6, the second-highest 40-over score ever at that time and it was great to see Vikram back to his best in that game, as he cracked 129 off just 89 balls. To be fair, that was all pretty inconsequential in the grand scheme as our early-season form had left us with too much to do, but it did mean that my own confidence in my leadership was growing.

There was definitely a burgeoning belief and collective purpose in our cricket in that period. It is perhaps not always appreciated by those looking from outside just how important it is for a captain to feel comfortable with his in-game thinking and thus be able to trust his decision-making at critical moments. When I became captain, even as an interim until the end of the season, though I believed in my judgement and tactical awareness generally, it was untested at that level of the game. By the time the last four-day game of the season arrived, at home to Sussex in mid-September, I was really enjoying the job.

Sussex had already had their promotion confirmed by that time and we were in third place, nine points behind Glamorgan. I lost the toss and my opposite number, Murray Goodwin, chose to bat on what was eventually to prove a somewhat unreliable pitch in terms of bounce, and one which later offered considerable help to the spinners. Rain curtailed play on the first day and more seriously on the second, at the end of which Sussex were still batting in their first innings on 225/7. At the start of the third day, Gareth Andrew snapped up the last three wickets in just eight deliveries, allowing us to get cracking quickly, as we had to, if we were to make a game of it. James Cameron and Vikram Solanki led the way as we reached 201/9 before I declared 36 runs behind and by the close, Sussex had extended that lead to 138 for the loss of two second-innings wickets. I knew that Murray was prepared to give us something to chase on the last day but even so the eventual target of 301 in 70 overs looked a tall order.

That we won at a canter, with 14.5 overs to spare, was down to a magnificent partnership for the second wicket between Moeen and James Cameron. Mo, in particular, batted at his glorious best, producing a number of comparisons in the media with another graceful left-hander, David Gower. He scored 99 out of 200 added between lunch and tea and reached his hundred off just 106 balls before eventually being dismissed for 115. James made what was, in fact, his only first-class century and we sealed a four-wicket win when Alexei Kervezee smashed Monty Panesar for six! There were some suggestions that Glamorgan, whom we pipped for promotion after they drew with Derbyshire in Cardiff, were disgruntled that we had manufactured a result but in all fairness our chase had been a properly contested affair and the win achieved through genuinely superb batting.

In some quarters, promotion was regarded as almost miraculous. All those departures by senior players, and what Bumpy bluntly called 'no funding', owing to the club's precarious financial situation, had not ultimately been allowed to deny a pretty youthful team (bar one or two glaring exceptions!) from taking something truly meaningful from what could easily have been a disastrous season. Quite justifiably, we celebrated long and hard.

I had made 1,180 first-class runs at an average of 42.14 whilst Mo had scored 1,260 and the blossoming Kervezee

1,190. Alan Richardson's 59 wickets were testament to his hard work and constant willingness, Matt Mason had taken 31 and the promising Richard Jones 38, so there was reason to be hopeful that this time we might be able to hold on to our top division status for more than 12 months. Bumpy was a coach who always made much of the idea that togetherness, the collective, that elusive and undefinable team spirit, was a 12th man and it was at times such as these that he liked to remind everyone of that belief. He said almost from the outset that we would look to consolidate in 2011 and made it clear that there were unlikely to be any huge overseas stars incoming. We would, he said, 'have to rely on the guys who got us here'.

My official elevation to the captaincy on a permanent basis was confirmed in my appraisal meeting after the end of the season but I think everybody knew that it was a mere formality. Although the initial circumstances at a very subdued Colwyn Bay had prevented me from really feeling excited at my elevation, as time had gone on I had begun to relish it. Under my leadership, we had won three and drawn one of the last four Championship games and my overall record was seven wins out of nine in all competitions.

As I departed with Danni for a winter playing club cricket in Auckland, I was perhaps more content than ever with my professional situation. That did not mean that I was taking it easy or felt that I could cruise along for a few years, but I was more than satisfied with where I stood when I honestly assessed my position. I had properly established myself as a county cricketer and, to the enormous pride of myself, my family and the Bret fraternity, I was captain of the Pears.

7

READY TO LEAD

NEW ZEALAND was a country Danni and I had always wanted to visit and I successfully applied to become the overseas player at Cornwall CC in Auckland for the 2010/11 season. Bumpy happily approved and having spent two consecutive winters at home I willingly took up the opportunity to play a decent standard of cricket and maintain my fitness in sunnier climes.

The arrangement with Cornwall was perfect for both Danni and me. We were given excellent accommodation, a good car and plenty of free time, whilst the club also fixed her up with a part-time job. We were able to benefit from a welcoming club atmosphere but also to travel fairly widely and to immerse ourselves fully into the culture of what is a magnificent country. Auckland itself, 'the City of Sails', is a vibrant and cosmopolitan place and within reach of some spectacular regions such as the Coromandel Peninsula and the Bay of Islands.

My form was good early on and I scored plenty of runs and even took a few wickets, so the club were quite relaxed when we disappeared from Sunday to Wednesday most weeks, before returning on Thursday so Danni could go to work and I could prepare for cricket on the Saturday. Though the pitches were not always that good, the standard of cricket was pretty competitive and, as in Australia, when our games did not coincide with the first-class programme you were very likely to play against the best domestic cricketers. All in all, it was just about the ideal working holiday.

Shortly before the end of the trip, I finally summoned the courage to propose to Danni. We had a day off and visited Auckland Botanical Gardens, an absolutely stunning place which manages to merge acres of native forest with various collections of plants, shrubs and trees from all over the world. I was all set to pop the question but then bottled it and decided to wait until dinner that evening. Again, I just didn't feel the situation was quite right, and suggested a post-dinner stroll to the top of Mount Eden, a beautiful volcanic hill which overlooks Auckland to take in the terrific view of the illuminated night-time city.

There I judged the ambience to be just perfect and romantically fell to one knee and managed to seal the deal at the exact moment we were joined by a busload of Japanese tourists!

I was, therefore, in a slightly different place as a person on my return from Auckland, preparing for married life in the not-too-distant future but certainly excited by the prospect of fulfilling my long-held ambition to lead Worcestershire. It would be a challenge but it was one I was ready to take on. My experiences of captaincy in youth and second XI cricket, as well as in Perth with Midland Guildford, had been good preparation for what lay ahead but I don't think anybody really knows whether they are cut out for the role of leading a county side through a complete season until they experience it. Towards the end of my time as a player, we started to see teams following England's example of having different red- and white-ball skippers, and it was an approach sometimes used at Worcestershire, but that was not what I faced in 2011. I was to lead the team in all formats but I think all concerned knew that the prime target was survival in Division One of the County Championship.

On reflection, I realised that Bumpy had been sounding me out to some extent for a season or two before Vikram's resignation as he had regularly sat with me whilst watching the game after I had been dismissed. As we observed our opponents' tactics he might ask, 'What would you do now if you were captain?' or 'Why do you think he's made that bowling change?' Another time it might be, 'What do you think he's trying to achieve by setting that field?' and although at the time I thought he was just engaging me in cricket chat I see now that it was what we might term 'succession planning'. Just a coach doing his job, of course, but yet another unseen aspect of the professional game which can slip by unnoticed by those not directly involved.

I had been shaped as a captain mostly by my predecessor and consider myself to be a similar character though perhaps with a different personality. Vikram enjoyed the utmost respect of all those around him and was generally quite a serious person. I absolutely shared his core values but was perhaps a more light-hearted and relaxed character and, consequently, more likely to be involved in dressing-room horseplay. However, it is obvious that with the same coach in charge and a new captain largely moulded by the previous incumbent, there was never going to be a fundamental change of direction. It was going to be a season of evolution, not revolution.

To say that you learn as you go along in captaincy is stating the obvious but trying to identify the influences is interesting, however difficult it might be to measure their relative impacts. I enjoyed watching opposition captains operate and occasionally discussing the game with them.

Kent's Rob Key, in particular, was always a guy whose approach impressed me; he seemed consistently proactive and creative in his thinking and I generally tried to be the same. Of course, it was very much a double act with the coach as far as the day-to-day running of the squad went, and we spent long hours in his office planning our strategies for different games, discussing team selections and generally mulling things over. Fortunately, our thinking was broadly similar and though we occasionally had different opinions regarding selection, he would usually say, 'Well you're the one that has to manage them on the field,' and my choice would be preferred.

One thing Bumpy and I shared was an absolute commitment to the Pears, and at every step of the way our motivation was what we believed to be best for Worcestershire. There are inevitably people who disagree with the decisions made by any coach or captain and that is probably a healthy thing as it stops any regime from becoming complacent or perhaps overconfident in its management. But I am more than satisfied that what was driving us at that time and beyond was a total dedication to the cause. The pride that I had always experienced when wearing the famous badge with its three pears was never more keenly felt than at that time and I am sure that I was working alongside a man who was equally, if not more, motivated by the same forces.

There is a widely held theory in sport that a captain needs to embody the three Cs, those being courage, care and consistency. Such neat labels might seem rather artificial but this one, I think, is born out of common sense.

I have already talked of bravery when it comes to batting against the quicks but the sort of courage demanded as a leader is completely different. I always tried to 'front up' when it mattered, whether that meant explaining to a mate why he had been left out of the team, delivering a dressing-down to an individual or the group, or facing the understandable inquest after a poor performance and recognising my own failings.

The caring part of captaincy is its least public component. To get the best out of a group, it is vital to regard each member as an individual though, of course, there's nothing original in me observing that some characters respond to the metaphorical carrot and others to the stick. What's not necessarily easy when you start in such a role is to identify the strengths and weaknesses of those around you so that you can start to implement your ideas effectively. Knowing what makes people perform best, what other pressures they might be feeling in their lives away from the game and, I guess, just who they are, takes time but is crucial, and going to the trouble of finding out those things shows that you care.

The third C, consistency, is equally vital. In any position of authority an even-handed approach is the only way to earn respect; all members of a team must be treated the same and standards which are set and expected have to be adhered to. I think I knew instinctively that it was important that I didn't change when I became captain, that I was still basically the same bloke I'd always been. There's no hiding place in a county cricket dressing room and if somebody, captain or not, attempts to present themselves as someone they're not they will be rumbled pretty quickly.

What I did become more aware of was ensuring that my example was at all times beyond reproach now I was captain. I was even more of a role model for the rest of the squad than before. This, of course, was especially true with regard to the younger players. That was never going to be an issue in terms of my general approach to training and preparation. My confidence had always come from knowing that I did things in the right way, a legacy of the example set for me in my early years by influential figures like Hicky and Bumpy, who continued to dedicate himself totally to the cause.

The work-hard, play-hard mindset was undoubtedly what I wanted to convey to the rest of the lads. I always liked to have a beer or two with my colleagues when appropriate, and while we certainly never embraced a drinking culture, I definitely consider it an important part of team bonding to socialise en masse from time to time. That absolutely does not mean that I approve of any pressure being placed on anybody to drink alcohol if they don't want to. I've already stated that this aspect of a cricketer's life had changed drastically since I entered the professional game, and indeed, it would continue to do so, but there's no denying that an occasional session with those that you play alongside can be hugely beneficial. It's really just a matter of knowing the right time and place.

Jack Shantry, at that time an ideal example of the sort of relatively inexperienced guy who would probably look to his captain for guidance, once made an observation which sums up my approach. He recalls a conversation I had with him in Bushwackers, our favourite Worcester nightspot, when I jokingly told him, 'Shants, it's very important with regard to drinking and cricket that you drink at the right time. You can also drink at the wrong time as well if you decide to, but you must drink at the right time!' And I suppose that just about sums it up.

I was never a captain who favoured extended team talks, preferring where possible to leave the detailed stuff, about how we intended to approach a game or what plans we might have for dealing with a particular opponent, to the coach, or perhaps making sure that such issues were discussed in team meetings, which took place the day before a game. In the modern game, of course, these matters have become very much the realm of the analyst. I tried to make my addresses to the group brief and meaningful, whether in the pavilion prior to a session of play or in an on-field huddle, generally reminding everyone of the need to concentrate and focus on their own individual roles. I found most players, though perhaps not all, generally quite switched on when it came to targets for a specific session or a powerplay.

I also attempted to draw on the experience of senior players. Mo was my vice-captain at the start of 2011 and though his motivational qualities, which later became massively impressive, were still embryonic, his energy and flair were vital. At that stage, he was by no means an accomplished public speaker and it was almost surprising to see that side of his character develop as he matured. By the time he was skippering the side in Twenty20 cricket a few years later, having banked an abundance of international experience, Mo was a compelling leader who could, with a few well-chosen words, inspire the group in remarkable fashion. He proved what I had always felt; that there is no need for a captain to attempt some sort of Churchillian masterpiece when what really works is getting across key points briefly and clearly.

Alan Richardson was another brilliant aide, assuming an almost unspoken responsibility for the leadership of the bowling group in the early period of my captaincy. Even though Matt Mason, as assistant coach with responsibility for that subgroup, was also very active, it was Richo upon whom I most relied in that department, certainly on the field. His vast and somewhat unusual experience, gathered at various counties and via what might be called a circuitous route, made him an almost unique influence. Ultra-reliable, invariably upbeat and in the form of his life, Richo was a joy to have in the side and it was reassuring to know that a unit of the team was basically looking after itself.

On the field, I always tried to be a proactive skipper. There are times when it is appropriate to persevere with a particular plan or approach, and patience is obviously a vital component of any team's armoury when it comes to taking ten, or indeed 20, opposition wickets but to let things drift is criminal. Mostly, I tried to make things happen, to be aggressive, to take wickets rather than contain and, especially in white-ball cricket, to drive home an advantage once established. When those instances occur in shorter games, as they invariably do, where a bowler is enjoying a fine spell but nearing the end of his allocation, the captain regularly faces that crucial decision whether to keep him going or save his last over or two for a later stage. In those scenarios, I would almost always keep the bowler going, believing it best to secure a position of strength.

One such episode which occurred late in my career springs immediately to mind, and it was in a game in which I was not playing. In our Twenty20 match at Headingley in 2021, I watched from the dugout as Dillon Pennington, our young quickie, produced an unbelievable opening burst, sending back Jonny Tattersall, Adam Lyth, Joe Root and Gary Ballance without conceding a run. It was a performance that won him the Worcestershire Cricket Society's 'Moment of the Year' award and his figures were an amazing 3-2-3-4.

Now I know hindsight is a wonderful thing and all that, but if I had been skipper, I would have kept him going and allowed him to bowl his final over whilst he was still in the moment. However, Ben Cox, who was captain, decided, understandably enough, to keep his last over back for the later stages, little knowing that by then the game would have drastically changed. Dillon's final six balls went for 21 runs as Yorkshire posted what proved to be an unassailable target. I offer no criticism of Coxy, who did what he thought was best, nor do I suggest that this one example justifies my philosophy but it does illustrate where my thinking comes from regarding such situations.

I generally felt that as a captain it was my job to make things happen. If I thought about making a bowling change or even an alteration to the field, I did it promptly rather than waiting. There is nothing more frustrating than thinking

'Shall I bring in another slip?' then deciding to leave it, only to see one of the next few balls fly at catchable height through the vacant space you were about to fill! In essence, then, my approach was to do, rather than to consider.

Setting fields is, of course, something you work on with your bowlers and some are easier to work with than others. Jack Shantry was one with whom I enjoyed a tempestuous on-field relationship and we regularly clashed over such matters. One incident he frequently recalls came fairly early in his career when he had, not for the first time, been clipped through the leg side for four. 'Mitch, could we have square-leg a bit straighter?' he asked. 'We could,' I shouted from slip, 'or alternatively, you could stop bowling bloody leg-stump half-volleys!' Shants was a wonderful, competitive character with a fiery temper but one who never took an in-play issue into the pavilion. He spent several seasons changing alongside me and any disagreements were always quickly forgotten.

I rarely resorted to issuing a collective bollocking, believing that such a tactic can only be of value if it is remarkable owing to its infrequency. Also, of course, you have to be careful because if you demand improvement from others, you've also got to provide it yourself. Many a captain has been more than a little embarrassed by getting out cheaply just after demanding some guts and application from his troops! One occasion, however, when I was sufficiently incensed to turn the air blue was at the Rose Bowl in 2013 and it is an outburst that I know is remembered for its vehemence by several of those present, which to some extent proves my point about not getting too upset too often if you want it to have an impact. Hampshire had piled up 500 with Jimmy Adams getting a double century and our reply was a mediocre 206. Even though we were fielding an inexperienced line-up, I ripped into them, spelling out in no uncertain terms that I wanted to see a bit more resolve and determination as we followed on. We still went on to lose the game, but thankfully my personal pride was intact as I managed a five-and-a-half-hour 92 in the second innings.

8

STAYING UP

AFTER A reasonably auspicious start in my new role, it was a bit of a shock to lose the first six Championship games of 2011 in the top flight. What was frustrating about this series of defeats was that in several of them we were, at some stage, in a really competitive position. In the first game against Yorkshire, we had them 155/7 in reply to our first-innings 286 but managed to lose by nine wickets. Then, despite a first-innings lead of 174, we lost to Warwickshire by 88 runs, before losing at Trent Bridge having compiled two totals over 300.

After a fourth reverse, this time at Taunton, I missed the next three games through the first serious injury of my career, leaving Moeen in charge, and it was he who led the team in the first Championship win of the season at home to Nottinghamshire. During my spell on the sidelines, caused by a side strain suffered whilst bowling in a 40-over game, there occurred what to this day remains the most bizarre sequence of events I have ever witnessed in cricket. Enter Adrian Shankar.

Shankar had appeared briefly at New Road some eight years earlier and had played three second XI games and made 55 runs at an average of 13. He had played largely unsuccessful second team cricket for Nottinghamshire, Middlesex and Sussex as well, before finally landing a two-year contract at Lancashire, where it seems, he did little really to impress. He also had a mediocre record for Cambridge University, where he had read law, and had made occasional unconvincing appearances in Minor Counties cricket for Bedfordshire. What happened next almost defies belief and, whether we like it or not, is a source of historical embarrassment for Worcestershire even though there was almost some comedy value in the episode.

There is some mitigation for Worcestershire's gullibility about what transpired, because, like all counties, we were desperate to strengthen our staff but had little money with which to do so. Yet there is no escaping the fact that due diligence was not carried out when it came to checking Shankar's credentials and both Bumpy and the chief executive, David Leatherdale, were left somewhat abashed.

The first I recall of it is a conversation with Bumpy during our game at Taunton in early May when he told me about a player who had been brought to his attention after some outstanding performances in a Sri Lankan domestic competition. Somebody had sent him the relevant, hugely impressive, statistics and he asked me if I thought it worth pursuing. I said that I remembered Shankar as a distinctly ordinary player from his days with us in 2003 but supposed that it was not impossible that he had gone away and made real improvements to his game. In the next few days, I got injured and then, two or three days after Shankar was signed, Vikram Solanki was badly hit on the head at Edgbaston by the giant Irishman Boyd Rankin, so Bumpy might well have felt that he had acted smartly as we clearly needed to find some runs from somewhere.

Shankar was given a contract until the end of 2012, and a press statement said that he had 'spent the winter in Sri Lanka gaining valuable experience and catching the attention of numerous counties'. He was reportedly the leading run-scorer in Sri Lanka's Twenty20 Mercantile League and had made 'three successive hundreds in the longer form of the game'. All of which sounded very good indeed. Adrian himself said, 'Having spent two seasons with Lancashire, I am delighted to be able to progress my career in county cricket. I am keen to make an impact and having spent the winter in Sri Lanka, playing in difficult conditions, I feel I am now better equipped to perform at the top level.'

What followed was shambolic. Vikram and I were both missing, but despite looking unconvincing in a net session and at fielding practice, Shankar was put straight into the side for a 40-over game against Middlesex at Lord's where he was bowled by Tim Murtagh for a third-ball duck in the second over. A heavy defeat ensued.

The following day saw his only inclusion in a County Championship match, against Durham at New Road. The visitors, a powerful outfit who had won the title in both 2008 and 2009, racked up 587/7 before declaring on the second afternoon and making early inroads into the Pears' batting line-up.

Adrian made his way out to bat with the score on 50/4 and 20 overs still left in the day. A genuinely hostile Steve Harmison was soon in full flight, backed up by, amongst others, Ben Stokes. He survived through to the close on 10 not out having faced 60 balls but was given plenty of reminders by the Durham bowlers and fielders that he looked a very long way out of his depth. Indeed, Gareth Andrew, who was batting with him towards the end of the day, recalls the fielders close to the wicket repeatedly referring to Shankar as 'Haydos', mockingly comparing him to the Australian batting legend, Matthew Hayden, who generally favoured playing off the front foot against even the very fastest bowling! With Harmison bowling seriously quickly, Adrian, completely at sea technically, was employing a big forward press to virtually every ball and could quite easily have been badly hurt. However, amidst considerable and widespread amusement amongst the fielding side, he remained not out at the end of the day's play.

The following morning Shankar appeared to suffer a serious knee injury during the fielding warm-up and had to be stretchered off by the medical staff and some of the other lads, meaning that he would take no further part in the game. The general feeling was that Harmison had put the wind so far up him that he simply didn't fancy resuming his innings. Another theory is that he'd become aware that investigations were being made into his cricketing pedigree.

That was the end of Shankar's career as a county cricketer. David Leatherdale, apparently alerted to some of the discrepancies in Shankar's story which were starting to emerge, including that he had lied about his age and had even completely invented the 'Mercantile League', cancelled his contract a few days later and the club even passed details of the affair on to West Mercia Police, who took no further action.

Subsequent investigations carried out by various journalists revealed if not quite the full extent of Shankar's deceptions, then still more than enough to characterise him as some sort of fantasist who had set his heart on a career in county cricket and was prepared to go to extraordinary lengths in pursuit of his dream. He was certainly 29 years old when he signed for us and not 26 as he had claimed. But that was far from the most startling of his falsehoods; he had basically created a virtual cricket career, complete with statistics, news reports and player profiles, in an attempt to dupe a professional club into taking him on. And let's be brutally honest, it had worked!

For a Cambridge law graduate of presumably fairly high intelligence to believe that he could actually carry off such a scam is surprising to say the least. As he had shown in one or two second XI performances across the years (including, incidentally, an innings of 41 for Worcestershire at Northampton in 2003) Adrian was not clueless as a cricketer, he just wasn't prepared, it seems, to accept that he hadn't quite got what was required to play at county level. I can't comment authoritatively on other claims he is said to have made, about hitting Sri Lankan legend, Rangana Herath, for five sixes in an over, of being on a life-support machine for the first three years of his life (hence the discrepancy regarding his age!) or being part of Arsene Wenger's first ever Arsenal academy intake, nor have I read in any detail the blogs he is said to have written about his own imaginary cricketing exploits.

I can report, though, that to those of us remaining in the New Road dressing room following his departure, the lasting impression was one of bemusement. In some ways, we felt part of something completely ridiculous but at the same time, we did not feel that we had actually contributed to it. It is impossible to ignore that the club's hierarchy had been made to look foolish and even though very little was ever said by them about it publicly, there must have been a feeling of distinct embarrassment. Even a cursory check of the facts would have revealed the frankly underwhelming statistics of Shankar's cricket in England over the previous ten years and would probably have precluded his inclusion in a first team fixture of any kind. It was a cock-up and it was followed by what was, if not a cover-up, a reluctance to talk about it which I think hid a hope that if it were never brought up in conversation, we could almost pretend it hadn't happened.

My side injury kept me out of action for almost a month but I was back in charge by the time we won our second consecutive Championship game, at home to Hampshire, and I was pleased to find a bit of touch with a couple of fifties. This game was also notable for a superb 173 from Vikram and a top all-round effort in his only Championship appearance by Shakib Al Hasan, who was on board for the Twenty20 stuff. Actually, my first-class form in that first full season as captain wasn't great – 751 runs at 32.65 with no hundreds being a modest return – and only Vikram passed 1,000 runs. I performed steadily enough in both of the shorter formats but we won only two 40-over games and finished two points off qualification after playing really well in the Twenty20 competition, which meant that our only chance of gaining anything meaningful out of the season was to retain our Division One status. That might seem rather an underwhelming ambition but to us players it was anything but.

We were a tight-knit bunch, well aware that we lacked the abundant resources of many of our rivals, and a mixed group in terms of age, experience and background. Over the previous winter, we had lost the services of Ben Smith, who had moved into coaching with Leicestershire, but there was the old war horse, Alan Richardson, the young and supremely gifted Moeen, the still elegant Vikram, the talented Dutchman Alexei Kervezee, and the battling all-rounder, Gareth Andrew. Throw in charismatic wicketkeeper, Ben Scott, who had come in from Middlesex, the Zimbabwean, James Cameron, the emerging Shants, Richard Jones, youngster Matt Pardoe and the variety of overseas players we utilised at different times, and a picture emerges of a fairly disparate collection of characters.

Whatever the chemistry was, it produced a brilliant dressing room environment in which it was a pleasure to spend time. Damien Wright, the Australian seamer who was with us for the first seven games of the Championship season, deserves special mention. I don't think I ever played with a more energetic and infectious character. Even though the records show that we lost six of the games he played, I believe we all agreed that he was a tremendously influential figure that year, and what we achieved after he had left us was partly down to him. That might seem a strange claim but those with experience of a team environment over a lengthy period are likely to recognise how it can happen.

Damien was loud, brash and funny. He could, it seemed, get excited about just about anything. I particularly remember a game at Taunton when his enthusiastic response to us being supplied with some decent but not particularly memorable grapes in the team's fruit bowl was quite something! He took 31 wickets in his seven games, a decent haul, but his impact was far greater because of the effect he had on those around him. To put it simply, cricketers, like everybody else, perform better when they enjoy going to work.

In such a battle to stay up every point is vital but it goes without saying that every win is priceless. We actually managed two more victories. The first came against Sussex at Horsham when Saeed Ajmal, who briefly replaced

Damien as our overseas player following Shakib's cameo appearance, took six wickets on the last day and we won despite Murray Goodwin's wonderful hundred. In years to come, when he returned for longer stints, Saeed showed us what an absolutely superb bowler he was, before problems with his action caused him to incur an ICC ban, but the part he played at Horsham was probably his single most important contribution in that first short visit.

Saeed also performed well in our improved Twenty20 campaign and, despite the fact that his English was not that good, he fitted in really well, being enthusiastic, committed and always keen to talk cricket. Alan Richardson took the other four Sussex second innings wickets, though it's probably his score of 41 in our second dig which deserves the most praise. Since Richo averaged about 10 across his lengthy career and only ever passed 50 once, this was a brilliant effort in a contest where the eventual winning margin was only 34 runs. We were hanging in there and though we lost the next two we were still hopeful of surviving in Division One when the leaders, Lancashire, came to New Road at the end of August and we produced what was probably our best performance of the season.

With our seam attack now supplemented by the Barbadian, Kemar Roach, another ebullient character, who had joined us to replace Saeed for the last few games, the wickets were shared around as we rolled them over for 161 in just 35.2 overs before reaching the close on day one already 48 runs in front. Former Pear, Stephen Moore, was absent when they batted for the second time as he had dashed away to join his wife who had gone into labour, and with Kemar bowling really quickly and Richo producing one of those magic little spells bowlers dream about, we cleaned them up for just 80. I think poor old Stephen was halfway down the M6 on his way back to Worcester when he got the call to say he needn't bother! Richo's 6-22 included five plumb lbws as he found an absolutely perfect rhythm, but that didn't stop us from enjoying a moment of high comedy in amongst it all.

For some reason the umpire, Peter Willey, in my time one of the very best on the circuit and well-known as a dour but also humorous character, had been upset by their wicketkeeper, Gareth Cross. When Crossy came out to bat, Peter jokingly said to me, 'Tell Richo to hit this bugger on the pads and I'll do the rest.' We all knew he was only kidding as he was far too fair an umpire to have even considered giving a batsman out when he wasn't, but even so when Crossy was trapped in front first ball we appealed enthusiastically. The truth is that Crossy was absolutely stone dead, hit smack in front and he'd have been on his way in any case, but that didn't stop us from collapsing into fits of laughter as the finger was duly raised! To this day, it remains one of my funniest experiences on a cricket field.

A ten-wicket win over the eventual champions was wrapped up in two days and, though we lost the last two matches, in the final analysis we had done just enough. We finished four points above Yorkshire who, along with Hampshire, were relegated.

When I retired ten years later, that was still the only time that Worcestershire had ever managed to avoid the drop from the top division since the inception of a two-division County Championship in 2000. It might seem strange to many but it certainly represents one of the highest points of my career and I know that others in that team still feel the same sense of achievement. We had succeeded in attaining our number one goal and done it against all the odds.

Our variety of overseas boys had claimed 69 Championship wickets between them but the real heroes of the attack were Alan Richardson and Gareth Andrew. Gareth played 39 matches in all formats and made outstanding contributions with bat and ball, not least in the Twenty20 competition. For weeks he carried a knee injury which eventually required surgery in the close season, but never stopped putting in his absolute all for the cause. His 52 wickets and 666 runs in first-class cricket tell their own story. It was no surprise that he ranked second in the country in the PCA's 'Most Valuable Player' charts.

As for Richo, it is hard to do justice to his efforts, and his inclusion as one of *Wisden's* Five Cricketers of the Year was richly deserved. Aged 36, he bowled 669 overs in first-class games and claimed 73 scalps, making him the top wicket-taker in Division One. He was accurate and reliable in any conditions, miserly on flat pitches and a real challenge for the batters on any surface that offered a bit of bounce or seam movement. I feel lucky that I had him in my team and that I could rely so heavily on him, not just to perform himself but to set a perfect example to the younger bowlers. I have always thought that Richo was a coach while he was still a player, drawing on his vast experience with three other counties. Jack Shantry, one of those who benefited from this, once said that Alan was 'confident but not ego-driven and made you feel better for being in his company'. Enough said.

9

YO-YO YEARS (2)

FOR THE remainder of my tenure as skipper we tended to bounce up and down between the two divisions in red-ball cricket, barring one year, 2013, when we stayed in Division Two. There were highlights certainly, both from a personal and a team perspective, and another promotion to enjoy, but we didn't win any trophies. And that is a part of professional sport that not all observers appreciate. Whether it's cricket, rugby, football or indeed any team game, only a small percentage of those involved as players, coaches, administrators or even supporters, enjoy the taste of true success.

Many clubs go for decades without claiming a trophy and it's not just possible, but even quite likely, that someone can have a lengthy and quite successful career without ever winning anything! Partly, what keeps them going is the possibility that it might happen, but perhaps the single most important factor is that they are earning a living playing a game they love. I honestly think most professional cricketers I encountered appreciated it was their good fortune to spend their working days pursuing a pastime that they started for fun. Even though it was a frustrating and exhausting grind at times it was for me always a privilege and a pleasure to be part of a full-time county staff.

Early in 2012 I got the chance to further broaden my cricketing experience with a couple of very brief stints playing in Zimbabwe for Mountaineers. Based in Mutare, in the east of the country, the Mountaineers were one of the franchises set up in 2009 when the domestic game was restructured in an attempt to raise standards. I did reasonably well in a four-day and then a one-day game at Harare, Hicky's original stomping ground, on my first trip in January but fared better when I returned for a slightly longer spell in February following a break in their domestic season to allow international cricket to be staged. The outward journey was memorable as I managed to find myself on the first ever Emirates Airlines flight from Dubai to Harare, where our arrival was greeted with some ceremony including water cannons and traditional dance! In one first-class game, against a Mid-West Rhinos team led by Gary Ballance, I hit 178 and 39 not out, and, with another decent knock of 94 a week later, I considered it time well spent.

The skill level was good but they perhaps lacked something by way of mentality. For example, there were bowlers who could bowl seriously quickly but they seemed to be without the experience to make the most of their attributes, and were generally predictable in their approach. Or there were quite capable batters who would throw their wickets away by getting caught in the deep off their first or second ball because they couldn't control their natural urge to attack. There was talent in abundance but an immaturity of method which, of course, the coaches were trying to address. It was a great cricketing experience, though, and I was impressed by the simplicity of the approach of the players who trained really hard, gave it their all on the field and enjoyed each other's company off it. It was, for me, notwithstanding my reservations about their slight lack of nous, pretty much cricket as it should be played.

I did have one quite frightening experience in Zimbabwe, which, on reflection, I might just have handled better. During a game in Masvingo in the south-east I contracted food poisoning and was rushed to hospital where I passed out while being assessed. I later woke up to find that I had been admitted and was connected to three separate drips! Having at one stage felt like I was going to die, I

My first bat

Beach cricket

Ready for action

Already trying to find a way

2005 – Starting out

2019 – Still smiling

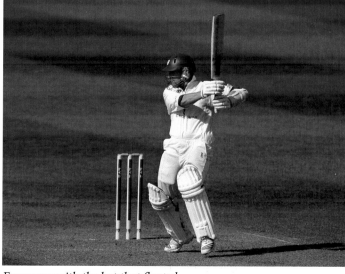

Four runs with the bat that floated

Missed this one from Lewis Gregory

And Lewis missed this one from me!

Finding the boundary at Edgbaston in 2015

Directing operations at Taunton in 2011

Under fire from Jofra Archer at Hove in 2017

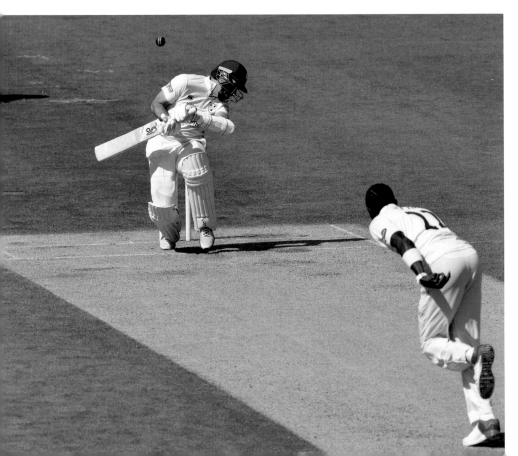

In one-day mode

I always took my T20 bowling seriously

Being inventive at Durham in 2015

Who said I was a blocker? A rare six in a rapid 45 against Somerset in 2020

The steer down to third man. Arguably my most productive shot.

Moeen Ali in full flow at Trent Bridge in 2012

Mo knows best. 2016

I'm in there somewhere!

recovered sufficiently to realise that I had, it seemed, been completely forgotten about. Eventually, after waiting hours to receive some attention, I recklessly decided to remove the various cannulas to which I was attached and just walked out of the hospital! Two days later, I was back on the field and apparently none the worse for the whole episode! I also escaped a speeding fine that week, courtesy of three cold cans of Coke in the back seat. The traffic officer who stopped me was clearly thirsty and excused the lack of cash in my wallet in exchange for a cool, refreshing drink in the midday sun!

Having worked so hard to retain top division status a year earlier, relegation in that wet summer of 2012 was a bitter pill to swallow but I think we all knew that we simply weren't good enough to repeat the heroics of 2011. Injuries to key players didn't help but the bottom line was that our batting wasn't anywhere near good enough. One statistic illustrated that fact – in only two of our 27 Championship innings did we pass 300.

Personally, I will always remember 2012 as the season that brought Phillip Hughes to New Road. Though I got on well with all our overseas players, I don't think I ever formed a friendship with any quite like that I had with Hughesy, and that's not an assessment coloured by subsequent tragedy. He was brilliant for us that year in all cricket, and particularly in Twenty20 where he averaged over 100, but it was just his general demeanour which impressed us all so much.

As suggested earlier you don't always have to win things to gain joy and satisfaction from team sport, sometimes just being alongside really good characters is reward in itself. I had a pal over from Cornwall, my club in New Zealand, that summer called Tim Wilson, though he was generally known as 'Chopper', for no reason other than because as a kid he had turned up to training on one of those legendary Raleigh kids' bikes of the 1970s. For some reason, he and Hughesy became really close friends. Chopper, who was a good but not brilliant cricketer, stayed with Danni and me in Worcester but played for Bretforton (who else?) at the weekends and he and Phil just hit it off right from the start. They regularly socialised together and I'd often get home from training to find Hughesy there enjoying a cup of tea with his new-found Kiwi mate! On reflection, although that season was a disappointment in many respects it remains one that I look back on with great fondness as perhaps one of my happiest.

What happened to Phil in November 2014, when he was struck on the neck at the Sydney Cricket Ground by a short ball, sent shock waves through the cricket world. His death, two days later, was especially devastating for those of us that knew him but was greeted with widespread horror by the entire cricket world. Phil was not the first player to die as a result of a blow from a cricket ball and, despite the improvements in helmet technology and design brought about partly as a result of his experience, it would be foolish to suggest that it could never happen again. In a game where a rock-hard missile is regularly projected at high speed there will always be risks. But for a high-class international batsman, wearing all the appropriate protective gear and somewhere near the top of his game, to be killed in such a fashion was hard to accept.

On the day he died, I recall being asked to do a series of media interviews in tribute to Phil and then just breaking down completely. I also couldn't help thinking of the dreadful effect the entire incident must have had on the bowler, Sean Abbott. I don't think there can have been a cricketer in the world who wasn't moved by what had happened but such tragedies are mercifully rare in the game and though they are, of course, warnings to us all to take all necessary steps to ensure our own safety and that of those with whom we play, they don't deter committed cricketers from continuing to play. Improved protective gear and more exacting concussion protocols have been introduced since that awful day and I know that now more than ever the game takes seriously its responsibility to protect its participants.

Inspired by Phil, we played our best cricket in that 2012 season in the shortest format and indeed, finished bottom of both Division One of the Championship and our section of the 40-over competition. In the Twenty20, though, we finished third in our group and earned an away quarter-final against Yorkshire having, remarkably, used the same 11 players throughout the entire group stage. Alas, their 212/5 was too big a target for us and we were soundly beaten.

Soon after the end of the season, in early October, Danni and I were married. I enjoyed a demanding stag do in Barcelona immediately after the cricket finished and then moved on, in the company of Vikram and Gareth Batty, to the nearby PGA Catalunya golf resort for the annual PCA golf trip before returning home for the nuptials. I can't claim that was the toughest week of my life but it did require me to draw upon the reserves of stamina built up through the punishing fitness regime I had followed for so many years!

Following that relegation Vikram, who had played such an important role in my development, left to join Surrey, Ben Scott retired and James Cameron decided to pursue a career outside the game. Though there remained several key members of that memorable 2011 bunch, it was yet another reminder that nothing stands still in sport.

One of the challenging aspects of captaincy, which I always enjoyed, was coping with changes of personnel. Overseas players, with their individual talents and quirks, came and went, as did a surprisingly large number of team-mates at one time or another. Increasing age, ambition, or lack of it, injury, and sometimes just plain failure to make the grade all play their part and the truth is that the demands of professional cricket are such that a player, if he is to survive, can't ever afford to mark time or stop working hard. There will always be someone after your place, a new pretender keen to impress, and that's exactly how it should be.

A look through the scorecards of those years tells an ever-changing story. The name D'Oliveira, so utterly iconic in modern Worcestershire history, appears once again, fleetingly in 2011, then more frequently in 2012 before Brett, son of Damian and grandson of the great Basil, became a regular who, of course, would go on to lead the county. Another future captain, Joe Leach, made his debut in 2013, more as a batsman than as the bustling seam bowler he would become. Ross Whiteley, one of the most brilliant fielders and dynamic strikers of a ball the club has ever had, arrived the same year, as did Tom Fell, and Ben Cox would soon be ready to assume the role of undisputed first-choice wicketkeeper.

On the other side of the coin, at the end of that season Richo called time on his fantastic four years at New Road. Bumpy wanted him to stay on but the offer of a coaching role at Warwickshire was perfect for him and the club reluctantly agreed not to stand in his way. It would be impossible to overestimate the role he had played but let's just point to his 258 wickets in that time to indicate how hard he would prove to replace.

Players move on, players come in and so the cycle continues. At any time, however, there are also those who remain, who are perhaps at that stage in their careers where they are just where they should be, mucking in, doing their jobs, maintaining their standards, trying to improve, just working at it, playing cricket, because that's what they do. And that was me throughout those yo-yo years, just getting on with being a professional cricketer, trying to score my runs, take my catches and perhaps the odd wicket, keeping myself fit, and making every effort to get all I could from my team. Win, lose or draw, Division One or Division Two, Group A or B, North Division or South, home or away it was all the same – what mattered most was that I was playing for the Pears.

Alongside me almost all the time was Mo. The world now knows what a great player he became and we at Worcestershire have been absolutely privileged to have seen him play some quite breathtaking innings over the years as well as produce match-winning spells with the ball. Perhaps less is widely known about him as a person and I am proud to count him as one of my closest friends in the game. He gives the impression of being fairly quiet and reserved generally, and certainly in his early days, he disliked media attention, though he became more comfortable with that as time went on. What people don't always see is what a sociable, fun-loving and mischievous character he is.

Mo is just one of those guys to whom people are drawn in a dressing room environment, and as his confidence developed as a player, so that bubbly side of his personality grew with it, to the point where he became an absolutely crucial figure. Along with Ben Scott and me, Mo became very keen on an addictive dice game called Perudo which I believe originated in South America. I can't even begin to imagine how many hours we have spent laughing, bluffing and teasing as we played. That was one pursuit where I have to admit I didn't always find a way to win!

One silly memory which never fails to reduce both of us to laughter concerns our very early days together when we regularly used to share car journeys. It must have been 2007 because we were travelling back from a benefit event for Vikram and I was driving. Our conversation turned to the possibility of being apprehended by the police for a motoring infringement and I very proudly told Mo that in my extensive four-year driving career, I had never attracted the attention of the law. Quite what the officer who apprehended me for speeding literally five minutes later made of the man laughing hysterically in the passenger seat we will never know!

There had been signs of Mo's extraordinary talent with both bat and ball for a few seasons but it was in 2013 that everybody began to see that we had a really special cricketer in our midst. It might have been an unremarkable campaign for us as a club but for him it was the year that propelled him towards international recognition. He piled up 1,375 first-class runs at an average of 62.50 with four hundreds, took 28 wickets and was named PCA Player of the Year.

I think that he had become aware that he needed to add something to his game to supplement his clearly outrageous natural ability and it was that realisation which made the difference. He improved his fitness and began to show a willingness to bat for sessions, perhaps scoring only 30 or 35 runs, in order to lay the foundations for a substantial innings. He spent more time practising, hitting thousands of balls with Bumpy, putting in some good, solid technical work to groove his strokeplay, and in the absence of a specifically dedicated spin bowling coach, he picked the brains of Saeed Ajmal and Shakib Al Hasan in order to improve in that area.

As an off-spinner, Mo had always been blessed with the ability to spin the ball hard, putting a lot of 'revs' on it, and with this as the cornerstone of his method he was able to add greater control and variation as he became more confident. He is a great example of a player who grew to understand his game and was then able to see where he could get better. That sounds easy but I have seen countless players who are unable to do that. If it were as simple as being told by a coach, 'Do this then do that,' and following those instructions then the world would be full of great players.

Of all those I batted with, Mo has to be my favourite partner out in the middle. Apart from the fact that he was generally relaxed and easy company it was just a total joy to watch him. Being the realist I am, I was never tempted to try and copy him, preferring just to enjoy the fact that the bowlers he was often unsettling were usually still struggling a bit when I got the strike and therefore unlikely to bowl me a 'jaffa'! That's a rarely discussed aspect of batting partnerships but an important one for us mere mortals. Some of his strokeplay was right up there with the finest I've seen, perhaps not quite as brutal as Hicky's or as graceful as Vikram's, but glorious in terms of timing, placement and inventiveness. We ran well together, too, often going on just a nod, a sure sign of a pair who trust one another.

Though he made many more highly significant contributions to the Worcestershire cause, it was inevitable that the further Mo went in the game the less he played for us. The result of his all-round progress was that he became an international superstar and enjoyed a fantastic Test career, as well as playing white-ball cricket in franchises all over the world, carving out almost the blueprint for a modern career profile. Though his globe-trotting exploits are about as far removed from my own one-club identity as it is possible to imagine, and his success limited the time he spent at New Road, I still regard him as a true Pear.

The 2014 season saw us promoted again and was a fine season for me personally as I racked up 1,334 runs at an average of 58 with five hundreds and was the fifth-highest first-class run-scorer in the country. Two tons in the game at Cardiff and big ones against Hampshire (172 not out) and Gloucestershire (167 not out), the latter in which I carried my bat, were highlights and, with Matt Pardoe's form stalling a little, I enjoyed the company of a new opening partner in the somewhat enigmatic Richie Oliver. Richie, who arrived from Minor Counties cricket, certainly played the game his own way and for a couple of years provided unpredictable but often effective contributions at the top of the order in all formats. However, his unwillingness to commit to spending winter working on his game in the UK, when he wanted to be in Australia, ultimately caused a parting of the ways.

For anybody associated with the club, though, the outstanding memory of that season has to be the home game against Surrey in September, or what has become known simply as Shantry's Match. The fact that the win sealed our promotion can easily be forgotten so remarkable were the circumstances. There are plenty of lengthy accounts in print elsewhere so I will not go into too much detail but will say that even for an experienced old pro like me with a lot to look back on, not many games come close to that one where turnarounds are concerned. It's one of those stories, like England's Ashes win at Headingley in 1981, that proves that in the game of cricket it really is never over till it's over.

I won the toss and chose to bat, then made a duck as we were dismissed for 272 before conceding a first-innings lead of 134 despite a brilliant effort from Shants with the ball as he claimed 6-87. Second time around, we were in deep trouble at 171/7 (yours truly having made 3) when Shants strode out to the middle to join Joe Leach. What followed truly was the stuff of dreams as Jack smashed an unbeaten 101 off 89 balls with 18 fours and two sixes, adding 108 for the eighth wicket with Joe, then another 71 for the ninth with the Kiwi, Mitchell McClenaghan. We set Surrey 217 to win and they had over a day to get them but with Mo, who incidentally made two fifties in the game, picking up three wickets, and Shants another four, we won by 27 runs. To make things just a tiny bit sweeter, perhaps, there were four former Pears in the Surry team in Vikram, Batts, Steve Davies and Aneesh Kapil. Shants had made 123 for once out in the game and taken 10-131. Wow!

That promotion, like those before it, owed much to the bowling unit and bore out my long-held belief that while batsmen sometimes win matches, it's bowlers that win titles or take teams to the top of league tables. Saeed's 63 first-class wickets were supplemented by 56 from Shants, 52 from relative newcomer, Charlie Morris, 33 from Joe Leach and 20 from a recovering Gareth Andrew. To be honest, leading that team in the field, with that attack, was relatively easy. As for white-ball cricket that year, the 40-over competition had been replaced by the new 50-over Royal London Cup and we made little impression, finishing seventh in our group, but I did feel that we were growing in our competitiveness in the Twenty20 format even if we once again performed disappointingly in an away quarter-final, this time at The Oval.

I was happy to sign a new four-year contract during the winter and enjoyed broadening my horizons again by joining an MCC tour to Japan in November before being selected for MCC in the traditional game against the champion county, Yorkshire, a day/night fixture held in Abu Dhabi in March. We Pears were once again prepared to have a shot at the higher level and I honestly don't think there was much more we could have been doing, as a club with our limited resources, to bring about success.

Even so, to call the next two seasons predictable, or unremarkable, is fair. We won only three Championship games in 2015, though crazily each was by an innings, and were, some would say unsurprisingly, relegated. Again, we were pretty dismal in the 50-over format, and yet again lost at the quarter-final stage of the Twenty20 competition, though this time in a rain-affected affair at home to Hampshire.

We were proving once and for all that we were that archetypal yo-yo club – too good to stay down but not good enough to stay up. A third-place finish in Division Two in my benefit year, 2016, after finishing nine points behind second-placed Kent, came alongside a slight upturn in form in the 50-over competition which brought another quarter-final reverse, but we did produce a less than satisfactory Twenty20 effort. So it was all very deja vu. Promotion, relegation, promotion, some players moved on, some players came in, an overseas star made a brief impression then another took over, there were a few white-ball wins here or there, a quarter-final defeat and so on. Perhaps the one difference during that up and down period was that we had seen an exceptional influx of young talent.

The key point to make here is that this was the reality of where Worcestershire were as a club at that point and indeed where most county clubs are most of the time! Inevitably such a repetitive cycle of existence is widely criticised. Members crave success and that means trophies, and even though cricket supporters are infinitely more patient than their footballing equivalents, dissenting voices are heard.

As captain I accepted the responsibility that I had to maximise the potential of the players with whom I worked, and I know Bumpy felt equally accountable. As a fiercely driven and passionate individual, he could upset some of the lads on occasions, but my own working relationship with him had remained very positive. I was still playing well enough and I actually believed strongly that we would make a real push for another promotion in 2017. I admit that at one point in 2016, as I searched my brain for a way to stop Leicestershire's batsmen from smashing our bowlers all around New Road, I did wonder if my time in charge was up but had quickly dispelled such negativity when we chased down 366 in just over 73 overs to win! And with Joe Leach, Ben Cox, Tom Fell and Brett D'Oliveira growing in maturity, and the likes of Ed Barnard and the dashing pair of batters, Joe Clarke and Tom Kohler-Cadmore, coming through, it really felt like we were on an upwards trajectory. I keenly anticipated having one more shot at Division One as captain.

What happened next was devastating.

10

WHERE THE HEART IS

LIKE MOST employees in professional organisations, county cricketers usually undergo an annual appraisal. When I turned up for mine on Monday, 26 September 2016, it's fair to say I was not expecting anything particularly earth-shattering. Despite the fact that we had missed out on promotion by a fairly small margin, it had not been a disastrous season by any means and though I had not had my best year my form had been reasonable enough, especially in the second half of the campaign. Having made a hundred in both innings of the game at Northampton in August when we had scored over 400 for victory – the second-highest chase in Worcestershire history – I felt secure, if not ecstatic, about my own game. It had been a busy year personally as I had been juggling the demands of family life, the captaincy and being the club's PCA representative as well as coping with all the commitments that come with a benefit year. However, my optimism regarding the squad's development, particularly in terms of young players, led me to believe strongly that we would be among the favourites for promotion next time around.

On reflection, I feel that I had changed slightly in 2016 and concerns regarding my own position had not been entirely confined to that rather frantic session when I had been trying to stop that assault from the Leicestershire batsmen. I had not had a good start to the season with the bat and I found myself becoming a little bit more reclusive than previously and perhaps worrying more about the many demands upon my time.

I wouldn't suggest that I was suffering from depression or the sort of serious mental health issues which have dogged many sportsmen, and particularly cricketers, in recent decades, but I was at one stage certainly feeling down and a little overwhelmed. I remember calling Danni from a hotel room in Derby and being moved to tears as I attempted to explain my state of mind. At her suggestion, I called the PCA's confidential helpline and found it helpful to unload my worries in conversation with an adviser before arranging a meeting with Tony Ghaye, a well-known psychologist whose services the club had acquired earlier that year. His input was especially helpful and I was able to implement what I might best term a reset in my thinking at that mid-season point which was definitely beneficial.

Applying a more realistic perspective and improved clarity to matters quickly turned things around and almost certainly contributed to my increased productivity with the bat in the latter half of the season. In later years my PCA work hugely broadened my awareness of players' mental health issues and made me mindful of the many challenges the game's support staff and administrators face in managing the welfare of its employees; my own difficulties, though relatively minor, have helped my understanding.

So, on that Monday morning in the coach's office with Bumpy and his assistant, Matt Mason, I sat and shared a fairly routine discussion about my season, covering my various roles in red- and white-ball cricket and assessing progress made or not made. As the meeting was nearing what I thought would be its conclusion I was told that they had decided that I should no longer be captain. For a few moments I was dumbstruck. I made it clear that I disagreed with the decision and felt that I deserved a chance to lead the side for what I genuinely believed would be a successful tilt at promotion, but it became clear that the decision had been made to replace me with Joe Leach and it was not up for debate.

It was suggested that the best course of action would be for me to resign but I flatly refused that option, believing quite strongly that had I gone down that route I would have looked like a quitter and that my true feelings regarding the matter would not have been widely appreciated. In essence, I refused to misrepresent the situation to my team-mates and the Worcestershire members with whom I had built a great affinity over the years.

In something of a daze, I went home to break the news to Danni, feeling angry and hurt. I made contact with Leachy and we went out for a beer the following night to discuss the situation. I felt absolutely no animosity towards Joe and was resolved to back him as captain come what may, and, in fact, I think our friendship was ultimately strengthened by the whole episode. However, I cannot pretend that I was not deeply affected by the experience. My childhood dream had ended in what I considered to be unsatisfactory circumstances and it would be wrong to pretend that my relationship with Worcestershire was not permanently damaged.

Subsequently I discovered that some of the other players already knew that I was to be removed from the captaincy, which was especially galling, and for some time afterwards I was in a fairly dark mood and was probably quite difficult to live with. Ultimately, of course, I was able to deal with the decision and to move on but it was not easy. I had, not for the first or the last time, been harshly reminded that professional sport is an unforgiving environment.

I felt to a certain extent that I had been made a scapegoat for the team's lack of success in 2016 and that the coach was making me the fall guy to deflect the pressures from above. His close friend and former team-mate, David Leatherdale, had moved on from his position as chief executive earlier in the year and I believed that Bumpy was feeling slightly vulnerable himself. That is a view that I was able to share in future conversations with him and it did not prevent us from making our peace in time, especially after I had given him a couple of pastings on the golf course. I certainly respect the fact that he made the decision with the best interests of the club at the forefront of his mind but the way that it was done, with no discussion whatsoever, was an issue for me.

In the immediate aftermath, I spent quite a time mulling over what would be my best approach when it came to responding to the inevitable media attention it generated. With hindsight I'm not certain that my decision to pen an open letter for disclosure on social media and other platforms was correct, but it was driven by a desire to tell the truth about the situation and to avoid multiple repetitive interviews. I felt that I had always been pretty straight with people so why change? I expressed my hurt and disappointment at the decision and made it abundantly clear that I had refused to resign, whilst at the same time thanking the coach for having given me the opportunity to lead the Pears in the first place. I also stated plainly that I respected the decision.

The news was made public on the Wednesday, two days after my appraisal, and the day of the PCA annual awards dinner, which that year was held at the Grosvenor House Hotel in London's Park Lane. Having rushed to complete my statement prior to travelling down by train I used the journey to begin drowning my sorrows, a process which continued throughout a fairly boozy evening. If nothing else, that served to make the night a little more tolerable as, not surprisingly, all anyone wanted to talk to me about was my sacking! It also became clear at that dinner that if I were to seek employment elsewhere, I would not be short of offers.

My open letter had been intended to make my position clear rather than to create a stand-off between me and the club or a personal confrontation with the coach, though that was inevitably how it was regarded in some quarters. Though I still had two years to run on my existing contract, the nature of county cricket is such that I had a staggering number of informal enquiries from other clubs regarding my willingness to move elsewhere. I dismissed a good few immediately as they were from counties which were, in my view, of a similar or lesser standing to Worcestershire, but several were of real interest, and the possibility of playing my home games in one of two or three Test arenas was certainly on the table.

One potential scenario would have seen me increase my salary by a huge margin into the bargain, but although a wage increase is never easy to turn down, as a family we were reasonably comfortable and to radically disturb our lives for financial gain didn't feel appropriate. Nor was it only domestic considerations which prevailed as my affinity to Worcestershire runs deep; family and friends are rooted in the county and my whole life to that point had been centred around its many qualities. Had I decided to pursue a move there might well have been contractual wrangles, compensation payments and other such complications, too, which could have further soured my relationship with the club and I would have hated that. And, though I had never set out to become a legend spoken of in the same breath as, say, Don Kenyon, Tom Graveney, Basil D'Oliveira or Graeme Hick I was still aware that I had led the county that counts them, and many others, amongst its great names.

I felt, too, that though winning a Championship title or another honour with a different county would be sweet, it would never compare to achieving something big with Worcestershire, and there was still that possibility. In summary, I just knew that whenever I considered playing for someone else my heart would always prevail and it was a case of 'Once a Pear, always a Pear'!

I had received a wake-up call, though, and the rest of my career was affected by it. I had always worked hard, tried to do the right thing by the club at all times, and showed loyalty. I had never really been difficult to please when it came to my contract, thinking that if I just got my head down I would receive my rewards somewhere along the line. Perhaps I harboured some vague notion of joining the coaching staff in some capacity when I finished playing. But things felt different from then on. I realised that my own position was perhaps not as secure as I had thought and reflected a little differently on the departures, some voluntary, some not, of one or two of my previous team-mates. Instantly hardened by the experience of being sacked as captain, my immediate response was to seek and secure a four-year deal, extending my existing contract by a further two years and guaranteeing my future at least in the short to medium term. In many ways, that drew a line under the matter and I was ready to move forward though it pained me to recognise that my romantic connection with the club had suffered irreparable damage.

When romanticism is removed, I suppose it is inevitable that it is replaced by cynicism, and I readily acknowledge that became a developing aspect of my character from then on. Whereas previously I had always gone out of my way for the Pears' cause, to welcome newcomers or offer advice to others, I became less eager to do so. At no stage did I ever become grudging in that area but I perhaps made less effort to seek out such opportunities.

As captain I had regarded it as an important part of my role to get to know the Academy players, the 'next cabs off the rank' so to speak, and I had been conducting weekly unpaid batting masterclasses in the winter months for the previous few years, but I concluded that arrangement, feeling slightly less generous regarding my spare time and input generally. I began to take a slightly altered view regarding my life after retirement, too, thinking that I perhaps needed to adopt a broader mindset, entertaining possibilities outside cricket and certainly beyond New Road.

I now recognise that the overall impact of the biggest setback of my life was beneficial; I had been guilty of allowing myself to become too comfortable and introspective and the shock of being reminded that I was dispensable was a valuable if painful experience. The course of my personal career had been one of almost unbroken progress when viewed from the perspective of successive milestones – village cricket, county youth programme, second XI, university scholarship, professional contract, first XI, vice-captain, captain – and I probably needed that bombshell to reawaken my ambitions in life generally. It dawned on me that my playing career would not go on forever and I resolved that over the next two or three years I would focus more on myself, my family and the development of skills and experience which might possibly assist me in a different life.

I have written previously of the importance of timing – remember the staff clearout perpetrated by Tom Moody in the winter of 2002/03 which created an extra place on the university scholarship scheme or the Stuart Broad no-ball at Grace Road in 2005. Well in February 2017 things fell my way again. Mark Wallace, who had just retired from playing for Glamorgan, was at the end of his tenure as chair of the PCA and the position became available. Had I still been Worcestershire captain I would not have considered putting myself up for election but as things stood, and after conversations with Vikram Solanki, a previous incumbent, and Wallace, I decided the time was right to stand. In Chris Rushworth of Durham and Oli Hannon-Dalby of Warwickshire I found the necessary proposer and seconder from amongst the other county reps and I was elected. Rushy probably felt he owed me a favour as I had surrendered my wicket to him so many times over the years! Dramatic as it sounds, that appointment and where it was to lead absolutely changed the course of my life.

11

A CHANGING OF THE GUARD

BACK IN the ranks once more, and perhaps with an increased focus on myself, I thrived, though not immediately. I had largely sorted out my differences with Bumpy, though my relationship with his assistant, Matt Mason, remained frosty for some years. I felt positive again and more than willing to throw my experience behind the new skipper. None of which helped me in the first couple of Championship games, when I scored 31 runs in four innings, 30 of which came in one knock! At first, I found it very strange being out on the pitch but not in charge, and I wasn't quite sure how to approach things mentally. Having spent so long, first as assistant to Vikram and then as captain, wrestling with on-field decisions, it felt strange just to stand at slip with nothing to think about other than the possibility of a catch.

Despite my own batting failures, we got off to a great start in the red-ball campaign. We won the first game away in Cardiff within three days and in some style. After dismissing the hosts for 207 on the first day, we recovered from 1/2 to make 403 in 94.1 overs with several of our talented rookies to the fore, including Tom Kohler-Cadmore who made a fine hundred. Then another youngster, Josh Tongue, making his Championship debut, picked up 5-45 as we knocked them over the second time around. It was a great start for Leachy and as we celebrated as a group with a few drinks after the game I remember thinking that it felt a bit like old times, albeit with a lot of fresh faces.

Big John Wayne Hastings (imaginatively nicknamed 'The Duke') had come in as our overseas player for the first half of the season and I thoroughly enjoyed his company and the positive impact he had on the young lads. There was a really positive buzz about the squad as we went on to a second win, this time at home to Northamptonshire, with the seamers hunting well as a pack. The confidence that I had felt about the prospects of this team when I had hoped for another year at the helm was proving well-founded.

What I needed personally was to start making some serious runs and thankfully, as May arrived, I hit some proper form. We had moved into the 50-over competition and I made 75 in a tied game at Northampton, then 69 as we beat Yorkshire at home before taking advantage of the chance for some practice in a Birmingham League Premier Division game for Brockhampton and hitting 194 off 151 balls.

It is tempting to dismiss something like that as an irrelevance and to suggest that league cricket is inconsequential for full-time professionals but that is to underestimate its value. For me the experience of playing a meaningful innings in a game is far more valuable than net practice and, perhaps because of my roots, I always enjoy such outings. In the next week I made 67 in a one-day game at Derby then my first hundred of the season in the home Championship innings win over the same opponents. My own season was well and truly up and running, the team was fulfilling its promise and optimism was certainly the dominant emotion in the camp.

My good form continued in the fourth successive Championship win which followed at Northampton. I made 161 in a six-hour marathon in the first innings and followed it up with an unbeaten 78 as we cantered to an eight-wicket victory. The Australian off-spinner, Nathan Lyon, had arrived for a brief four-match stint which gave the side a powerful boost and certainly helped to maintain impetus, and the seam attack continued to fire. Leachy's aggressive style, based on a threatening wicket to wicket line, was ideally complemented by the remainder of the group with Ed Barnard's variations, Shants's left-arm angle and the ever-improving Josh Tongue's pace making the overall unit one which offered a constant threat owing to its ample variety.

Though we lost the next Championship game at Hove, the one I referred to earlier when I discussed bravery in the face of seriously quick bowling, I managed a hundred and a fifty and then, following two failures in another defeat, this time at home to Glamorgan, I hit 142 in a big winning run chase at New Road against Kent which put our season back on track. Two draws and a loss, again to Sussex, meant that though we were still in the title race going into the final third of the season we needed to improve and we did so in style. Four successive victories propelled us to the Division Two title and my own consistency in amassing 508 runs in eight innings across that spell played no small part. That included three more centuries, one of which, an unbeaten 139 at Trent Bridge in early September, I regard as my finest ever innings.

In challenging conditions on a seamer-friendly pitch it was a relatively low-scoring game and seemed very much to be going our way until a ninth-wicket partnership of 56 between the Nottinghamshire skipper, Chris Read, and tail-ender Jake Ball threatened to take it away from us. Eventually, despite the outstanding combined efforts of Leachy, Ed and Josh in bagging 19 wickets between them, we were set a challenging target of 226. The varied Notts pace attack of Brett Hutton, Jake Ball, Harry Gurney and Steven Mullaney posed lots of questions and for us to triumph by eight wickets was a superb achievement. My unbeaten effort was in some ways uncharacteristic, given that my role in contributing to team totals had traditionally been as something of an anchor rather than a dominant figure, but it was one of those occasions when everything just seemed to come together, perhaps best illustrated by the fact that I even managed to clear the ropes on two occasions! My assessment of that knock as my best ever is partly coloured by the feeling that it was the cornerstone of a victory which went a long way towards sealing top spot.

The new captain had every right to feel satisfied with his work. In winning nine of our 14 Championship games we had finished 16 points clear of second-placed Nottinghamshire, racking up more batting bonus points than any other side whilst also collecting a more than healthy 39 bowling points and made the most of the qualities of the three overseas bowlers who had been at his disposal at various times. The acquisition of the brilliant Indian off-spinner, Ravi Ashwin, who had made vital runs and picked up 20 wickets in those last four games had been a masterstroke by the management. Given the qualities of the squad that year I could not help somewhat grudgingly feeling that things wouldn't have been much different had I still been in charge but that is not to detract from what Joe had achieved.

Having played in every Championship fixture, I made 1,266 first-class runs and scored seven hundreds, the most since Tom Moody's similar effort 21 years previously. I was more than happy to have responded so positively to what had been such a huge personal setback the winter before. To be voted as Players' Player of the Year also meant a great deal as it reassured me that I was still held in high esteem by my colleagues despite my reduced status.

In white-ball cricket it had, however, been a year of mixed fortunes. We were exceptional in the Royal London 50-over competition, winning six of our eight games to finish top of the North group, before being absolutely walloped by Surrey in a home semi-final, but our Twenty20 campaign had been dismal. There were highlights, none more memorable than Ross Whiteley's six sixes in an over off Yorkshire's Karl Carver at Headingley, and some brilliant individual efforts, notably from Joe Clarke, whose 124 not out off 53 balls at home to Durham was simply breathtaking, but to finish eighth in our group was very disappointing.

This was especially true given the batting firepower we had in our line-up which included the ebullient Clarke and the powerful pair of Whiteley and Hastings, though sadly no longer Tom Kohler-Cadmore who had defected to Yorkshire in mid-season. What we lacked in that format, I think, was a clear and consistent strategy such as we developed in the successful years that followed and proved that as a collective, we were learning. My own batting experiences in the 2017 games illustrate the point; half the time I was opening, sometimes I went in at No.4 but also at six, seven and nine. Obviously, in-game flexibility has to be taken into account but in our largely fruitless search for a winning formula we too often lacked a repeatable plan.

The following December came arguably the single most significant event of my entire career from a Worcestershire perspective, when Steve Rhodes was removed as director of cricket. The circumstances surrounding the decision are well-documented and there is very little I can add to what is already known. Having been made aware of an allegation of rape against one of our players, Alex Hepburn, in the preceding April, Bumpy chose not to inform the club's hierarchy and he paid dearly.

I am absolutely convinced that he acted in what he considered to be the best interests of all concerned in withholding the information, but it was an error of judgement on his part and the club management obviously considered that it had no real alternative but to pursue the course of action it did. Had David Leatherdale still been Worcestershire's chief executive when the allegation was originally made, things might possibly have turned out differently. David had a very close connection with the coach and if he had been made fully aware of the situation, could possibly have advised him more appropriately, whereas it was no real secret that Bumpy and Tom Scott, the interim CEO at the time, did not enjoy the same working relationship. Although I was by then chair of the PCA, I had no involvement at all as, quite clearly, I was regarded as having a conflict of interest.

In any event, it was a sad way for the absolutely magnificent contribution that Bumpy had made to the club over a period of 33 years to come to an end. As a wicketkeeper he holds the record for the most dismissals for the county in first-class and List A cricket, both tallies that will almost certainly never be beaten. His playing career spanned 20 seasons and he was essentially the architect of the club's modern playing image. As I have already suggested we did not always agree, and on the odd occasion he could be an awkward and extremely demanding character to work under or alongside, but his absolute dedication to the county makes him one of the single most important figures in its history. On top of that I would add that I owe him an enormous debt of gratitude for so many of the things I achieved as a player.

The players were generally saddened and somewhat shocked by the turn of events but the club acted quickly to install another Yorkshireman, the universally popular Kevin Sharp, as head coach. With Bumpy's assistant, Matt Mason, making a move to Leicestershire, bringing Alan Richardson back to New Road as the bowling guru was also a smart decision, and the new coaching staff was completed when Alex Gidman, who had joined us as a player in 2015 only for a finger injury to abruptly end his career, returned to take charge of the second XI.

12

REWARDS

HAVING MOVED on completely from the shock of my sacking, and off the back of my best ever season, preparing for the summer of 2018 under a new regime was exciting. Nonetheless, at the age of 34 and recently awakened to the need to look ahead, I was becoming increasingly aware that I might well be one of those cricketers who never really gets his hands on much silverware. The Pro40 win of 2007 was a dimming memory and, having passed up the opportunity of moving to another county perhaps more likely to be a candidate for top honours, I, perhaps more than most of the lads, craved a trophy. The second division promotions we had won with such frequency were each highly commendable and represented much in the way of hard work, both individually and collectively, but I think we all knew that they weren't the real thing, so to speak.

Another relegation from the top division of the Championship showed that you can make all the changes you like in terms of coaching staff and captains but in the longer form of the game, and over a full season, the harsh reality is that if you're not good enough you won't survive. We won only two of our 14 matches whilst losing ten, and finished bottom of the table, a full 29 points adrift of Lancashire.

There were, of course, some good sessions and the two wins we did manage, over Lancashire at home and Yorkshire at Scarborough, were both achieved by enormous margins, suggesting that when we managed to put several sessions of dominance together, we were a decent outfit. But how many underachieving teams can trot out that old chestnut? We all knew that the consistency of performance that we constantly called for was easier to talk about than to produce, and in the final reckoning we simply weren't competitive enough.

My own season, with four hundreds including one in either innings in the win over Lancashire and a big one at Scarborough, had been decent, but losing Joe Leach to injury fairly early on had hurt us, and overall, we had no complaints at the way things turned out. The innings win over Yorkshire at the seaside was especially memorable for me as I shared a massive partnership with my old mate Moeen, who was making a rare first-class appearance for us. We added 294 for the second wicket as I made 178 and Mo hit 219, and the reception we received as we left the field at the close of the second day was something I shall never forget. We were both unbeaten and had each passed three figures, and as the home crowd in that unique ground rose to us it was one of those rare magical moments which make all the hard graft seem worth it!

The challenge of playing successfully in the different formats of the county game is one with which coaches, captains and players have wrestled since the introduction of one-day cricket in the 60s. As the various different versions evolved, spawning a host of new skills, laws and terminology, the conundrum became increasingly complex. We became familiar with pinch hitters, switch hitters, reverse lappers, death bowlers and powerplays. The kits changed colour, as did the balls and the sightscreens, and even the names of the teams were altered. But the problem remained – how do teams, often largely comprised of the same individuals, play consistently well when the format of the game keeps changing throughout the season?

From the late 60s through to the 90s a season-long 40-overs-per-side Sunday League competition was a hugely popular cornerstone of the county programme and Worcestershire's wins in 1971, 1987 and 1988 count among the club's most treasured honours. Generally, it was customary, I understand, to start a Championship game against an opponent on, say, a Thursday or a Saturday, then to break off and play the Sunday League game against the same opponents, usually on the same ground but on a different pitch. A mat of some description would be used to cover the strip being used for the longer game, which would resume the following day.

Such arrangements now seem completely bizarre but the requirement to switch, literally mid-match, from one type of cricket to another was commonplace. In those days they also had, of course, two other longer limited -overs competitions dotted throughout the season. Then, with the demise of 40-over cricket and the advent of Twenty20, there came about various well-meaning attempts by the game's administrators to separate the playing calendar into single-format blocks. This was partly to make it easier for players to adapt to the specific demands of those different formats but also to maximise the marketability of competitions such as the Twenty20 Blast, which is far more likely to grab and hold attention if it is played in a concentrated period.

No solution satisfactory to all is, I fear, ever attainable. If white-ball cricket, as it has become termed in the modern era, is to be played in England and Wales in the high summer when it is most likely to attract good crowds, then some of the red-ball stuff is necessarily pushed to the start and end of the season. The consequence of this, and I speak from the heart as an opening batsman, is that scoring first-class runs is difficult and we are less likely to develop the batting skills required for success in the Test arena. This is, of course, not a new argument and not one likely ever to be resolved as long as financial and technical imperatives are in direct opposition.

My point in including this debate at this juncture is that we at Worcestershire had long wrestled with the red-ball white-ball dilemma. Focus too much on one and the other suffers but apply insufficient attention to either and everything can fall apart. Welcome to the world of the county cricket coach! Some clubs have experimented with separate coaching groups for different formats, and increasingly as my career drew to its end, I saw counties fielding teams with as many as six or seven personnel changes depending on the type of game.

In that 2018 season, when we won only two red-ball games, we played probably the best, most consistent white-ball cricket of any team that I was ever part of. We again won our group in the Royal London 50-over Cup only to suffer an agonising semi-final defeat at home to Kent, despite posting a score in excess of 300 thanks to a brilliant innovative unbeaten hundred from Ben Cox and an equally impressive fifty from Ed Barnard. To lose that one with just two balls remaining and to miss out on a Lord's final was really tough to take and while I wouldn't say my hopes of winning a trophy with the Pears were dying, I was beginning to ask myself how many more opportunities there might be. However, as we moved into July and at last found that elusive successful and repeatable plan in Twenty20 cricket, along with a young death bowler called Pat Brown, I sensed there might yet be reason to believe.

In the previous few seasons, we had always had the strength in our batting to make competitive scores in Twenty20 cricket, thanks to the quality of a number of our overseas imports allied with some of our own power hitters, but had frequently fallen short of the standards required to win tight matches when it came to our bowling in the closing overs. Though we tended to perform quite well with the ball early on and in the middle overs of an innings, that ability to restrict opponents' scoring opportunities towards the end had always been a problem.

So-called death bowling is perhaps the most difficult of skills for a bowler to master. At various times throughout the evolution of tactical strategies in the shorter forms of the game, coaches and bowlers have tried a variety of approaches to this crucial aspect of team performance. The ability to bowl frequent yorkers has always been valued, subtle changes of pace and a variety of slower balls are effective and the use of very full, wide deliveries has become more common. That season, our pace bowlers, Ed Barnard, Wayne Parnell, Luke Wood and, in particular, the young and relatively inexperienced Pat Brown, went some way towards mastering the art of restricting batters' scoring options in the later overs.

Wayne, a South African left-armer, would often bowl around the wicket to right-handers, thus hampering their chances of freeing their arms for big shots, while Barny used a wide variety of deliveries to make him unpredictable and therefore difficult to dominate. Luke, at that stage a vastly underrated all-rounder and another left-armer, who had come to us on loan from Nottinghamshire, was also one whose willingness to mix things up made him awkward to bat against while in Browny we had uncovered a gem. Tall, and sharp enough to generate considerable bounce without ever being really quick, he developed a wonderful range of variations of pace which for a couple of years genuinely bamboozled opposition batsmen and eventually saw him gain international recognition in the Twenty20 format. Of all Pat's attributes perhaps strength of character was his greatest; he was cool under pressure and his resilience had been enhanced by the experience of bowling the last over in the 50-over semi-final defeat against Kent.

Putting the huge disappointment of that loss behind us, we began the Blast campaign with a brilliant five wicket win at Old Trafford, chasing a target of 189 and getting home with one ball to spare. Wayne Parnell had yet to arrive but we were blessed with the presence of two fine overseas batsmen in the dynamic Kiwi, Martin Guptill, and the experienced Australian, Callum Ferguson. Both offered tremendous experience and different but highly complementary skills. Guppy was an explosive ball striker and always likely, at the top of the order, to get us off to a good start while Ferg, as he had already demonstrated in the 50-over competition, was a master of pacing an innings and more than capable of completely dismantling a bowling attack. My own contributions were predominantly with the ball and, though I rarely bowled a full four overs, I was comfortable turning my arm over at any stage in an innings and I'm certain my efforts were valuable.

Three consecutive victories followed the first and the side, being led at that stage by Brett D'Oliveira, was pretty settled both in terms of personnel and performance. It's never easy to put your finger on exactly why something as nebulous as good form in a team setting just 'clicks' but when it does, it's an absolute pleasure to be part of it. Each member of the side seemed to know exactly what their job was and we were able collectively to remain calm and focused under pressure. Of those first four wins, two were achieved when we batted first and two when we chased – a sure sign of a team that is confident.

Two losses followed but four more wins came next, and though Guppy had left us owing to other commitments, his loss was compensated for by the return from his other duties of the talismanic Moeen, who took over the captaincy. Durham were despatched at New Road thanks to a brutal onslaught from Ross Whiteley whose 60 off just 26 balls allowed us to overhaul their excellent 194, then a sensational 56-ball hundred from Ferg helped us trounce Notts at Trent Bridge.

Wayne Parnell had by then arrived and despite Mo's absence for two outings and a couple of losses, the ship not only remained on course but promising patterns were developing, particularly in terms of the way we used our bowlers. A majestic 115 off 56 balls from Mo, which included seven sixes, saw us to a winning total of 209 in the final group game against the Bears and set up a home quarter-final against Gloucestershire. Though I hadn't really had the chance to make many runs, generally being down on the card to bat at No.9, I had been bowling my two or three overs in almost every contest and I was absolutely buzzing as the next stage approached.

With the opportunity to reach finals day for the first time in the club's history and perhaps knowing deep down that I might never get another chance, I don't think I have ever been as nervous before and during a cricket match as I was for that quarter-final. Mo won the toss and decided we'd have a bowl, a decision which wasn't looking all that good when their openers, Miles Hammond and Michael Klinger, had steered them to 63 without loss after seven overs.

At that point, Mo threw me the ball, and after conceding a couple of singles off my first three deliveries I trapped Hammond lbw. Though it was my only wicket in the innings, I went on to produce one of the tightest spells I have ever managed in Twenty20. It was decided that as long as my slow stuff wasn't being targeted, I would keep going and thus I bowled my full four-over allocation straight through. Finishing with figures of 4-0-15-1 and having conceded nothing other than singles, I was absolutely thrilled with my performance and, though I was never one to be particularly demonstrative in showing such emotion on the field, I was beyond satisfied. With Brett chipping in with a miserly and damaging spell of 4-0-24-4 and Parny bowling his four overs for only 22, our combined effort in restricting them to 136/8 was magnificent.

It's probably fair to say we made heavy weather of the chase. We lost Mo in the second over, then Joe Clarke in the fourth, and at the halfway mark we were in some trouble at 55/3. Given that at the same stage they had been

76/1, the size of the challenge ahead was clear. Hidden away in the changing room, I was almost unable to watch. Ferg, however, brought to bear all his experience and was calmness personified as he steered us home with a measured unbeaten 64 off 47 balls, helped, it must be added, by Ross striking two sixes in a rapid 20. The win came with ten balls to spare and the dressing room celebrations were understandably joyous. We had been one of only two counties which had never been to finals day and the long wait was over!

Kevin Sharp's overall approach as head coach was fairly relaxed and supportive whilst also shrewdly delegating responsibilities to his staff. So it had been Alan Richardson and Alex Gidman who had taken most of the responsibility for our white-ball cricket that year though Sharpy had quietly and calmly overseen it all. I have made mention of the shining lights in certain performances but in truth, it had been very much a collective effort which had got us through to what had by that stage become domestic cricket's biggest day of the year, always played out in front of a packed and raucous Edgbaston. In all, we had used 17 players in the entire tournament but there had been a core of seven or eight constants within the team and each had done something crucial at one point or another. It must also be remembered that even those who played just three or four games, like

George Rhodes, Dillon Pennington, Andy Carter and Tom Fell, had all contributed significantly.

We lost three Championship games between the Blast quarter-final and the big day and though I wouldn't say that anybody's concentration was deliberately elsewhere, it was completely understandable that some of us were slightly distracted by what lay ahead. After the third of those defeats, we had one day to switch mindset and practise for Edgbaston and I recall feeling reasonably calm, and certainly nowhere near as nervous as I had been before the previous round.

Mo talked very positively to the group on the eve of finals day and his message was clear and unequivocal – we were not going to make up the numbers, we were going to play not one but two games of cricket, and the skills which had carried us this far were going to take us all the way to the title. I have referred previously to the remarkably galvanising effect which he always had on the team by that stage in his career, and it was never more evident than in that fairly brief address. I believe that he had learned a great deal from his time with England under the stewardship of Eoin Morgan in that respect. Morgan is, by all accounts, a truly inspirational leader and I have no hesitation in applying the same label to my old friend.

The effect of his words was almost palpable. In my view Mo was without doubt our best player in all forms of the game, and certainly in Twenty20 cricket, but what he did more than anybody else I've ever seen was bring out the very best in everybody else. His ability to inspire others to be 10 or 20 per cent better was indisputable and I am convinced that some of the performances turned in by the likes of Pat and Coxy, who were just sensational in that period, would not have been possible without him. How a colleague, a captain or a coach actually manages to instil that level of belief in others is one of those aspects of team sport which is impossible to explain, since it depends on so many unquantifiable factors, but when it happens it is priceless.

Remarkably, having explained how tense I had been during the quarter-final, I never felt any nerves at all on finals day itself. As part of the first Worcestershire team ever to get there, I was just determined to enjoy the whole occasion. I have often thought that for a county player like me, whose experience doesn't include any international or major franchise cricket, the Blast's climax at Edgbaston in what by then had become a televised extravaganza played in what could be termed a carnival atmosphere, was as good as it gets, almost like being a Premier League footballer for just one day. The hype, the electric atmosphere and the fact that the focus of the entire cricket nation was on us made it an almost surreal experience, and it was a day like no other.

Our semi-final against a powerful Lancashire line-up was the first game of the day and began at 11 o'clock. We lost the toss and were asked to bat on a pretty tacky pitch which we expected to improve as the day progressed, in keeping with what had happened at the ground in previous years.

We made a good start thanks mainly to Mo but after he was dismissed for 41 off just 21 balls, we lost two more wickets without adding a run to find ourselves at 70/4 in the ninth over. Ross Whiteley perished going for a big hit and I joined Coxy in the 11th over with the score on 82/5. Having nurdled six runs off ten balls, I went too far across my stumps trying to run a ball from Jordan Clark behind square on the leg side and was lbw, and with just 97 on the board off nearly 14 overs, we were in need of something special if we were to post a meaningful target. That something was provided by Coxy, who enjoyed possibly the finest day of his career to that point, and Ed Barnard. Together, they played an array of brilliant shots, mixing innovation with power hitting, to plunder 72 runs off the remaining 38 deliveries and took us to 169/6 – not a huge total but one which we felt gave us a fighting chance.

Lancashire had a threatening array of batting talent, including the exceptional hitting potential of Liam Livingstone, Jos Buttler and Dane Vilas, and their reply began brightly but once Livingstone fell for 30 to a good tumbling catch by Brett off Barny, we gained control. Mo bowled superbly, removing Arron Lilley and Buttler in a spell of three overs that went for a mere nine runs, and eventually we got home comfortably, winning by 20. The skipper finished with figures of 4-0-16-2 and Pat picked up the last four wickets to return 4-0-21-4. I bowled just one over, the 14th, and conceded 13 off it but I took a decent catch in the deep and thoroughly enjoyed the whole thing. I spent much of the day fielding in front of the famous Eric Hollies stand, taking in the entertaining chants of the crowd as they became steadily more inebriated and marvelling at the antics of the various groups in fancy dress as monks chased nuns while Batman and Superman pursued Donald Trump!

Sussex amassed a score in excess of 200 to comfortably beat Somerset in the second semi-final and so we went into the final, which began at 6.45 in the evening in front of a crowd nearing the peak of its collective delirium, knowing that we would need to be somewhere near our best. Remember, we no longer had Guptill or Ferguson in our ranks, but what we did still have at the forefront of our minds were the words of Mo from the day before!

Again, we lost the toss, but this time we faced the prospect of batting last, under the lights as the dew fell. Our opponents made a lively start, and with Phil Salt smashing two consecutive sixes off Wayne Parnell in the second over, the score was already on 19 when he pushed the last ball to Dolly at backward point and went through for what looked as though it would be a regulation single. However, as Brett's throw hit the stumps at the non-striker's end and several of our players appealed hopefully for an unlikely looking run-out, the video replay showed quite clearly that, though Salt was well past the crease when the ball struck the wicket, neither of his feet, nor his bat, were in contact with the ground and he was therefore out.

It was one of those moments where you just wonder if it's your day. Nonetheless, Luke Wright, who had smashed 92 in the semi-final earlier in the day, and Laurie Evans, both found the boundary fairly frequently in the next few overs and the score was 77/1 halfway through the tenth over. Mo, as usual though, was calmness personified and he produced a beautiful turning off-break to bowl Wright for 33. Evans was then joined by the flamboyant Delray Rawlins and the pair added 44 in the next four overs (one of which I bowled, conceding 11) before our inspirational leader struck again, removing Rawlins for 21.

Thereafter our seamers stepped up in admirable fashion and, despite Evans's fifty, only 36 runs came off the last six overs, two of which, overs 17 and 19, Browny managed to bowl whilst conceding just nine. His final analysis of 4-0-15-0 was just incredible for one so young; his command of

'ONCE A PEAR ...'

an array of different slower balls being his chief weapon as he outwitted those who tried to get after him. The final score of 157/6, though competitive, was far from unassailable and we felt quietly satisfied at half-time.

Joe Clarke and Mo got us off to a fine start in reply and the score had reached 61 when Joe was out for 33 in the seventh over. The wickets of Tom Fell and Dolly both fell fairly quickly before Mo was caught at long-off for 41 from 27 balls in the 12th over we were 96/4 off 13 and required 62 at nearly nine an over. When Ross was brilliantly caught by Chris Jordan off a Jofra Archer full toss we still needed 32 off 19 deliveries, the atmosphere was frantic and the noise level unforgettable as strains of 'Hey, Jude' and 'Sweet Caroline' filled the air.

That combination of circumstances, and perhaps his form earlier in the day, sent Coxy to unparalleled levels of achievement. Just why a player gets into the zone, as players call it, nobody really knows but on occasions individuals manage to find within themselves the levels of focus, calmness and skill to produce something truly memorable and this was Ben's time. Facing one of the best death bowlers in world cricket at that time in Chris Jordan, Coxy hit a four and a six as 14 came off over 18. Archer, capable of express pace, was to bowl the next, with 17 still required. Barny got a single off the first ball then Jofra, presumably trying for a yorker, got it wrong and sent down a beamer which missed everything, including the wicketkeeper's dive, and went for six no-balls!

I can only imagine the levels of adrenaline coursing through Ben's body as he cracked the ensuing free hit over backward square leg for six, and when he followed that up by swinging the next ball for four we had won, amazingly, with nine balls to spare! Coxy's 47 not out off 27 balls with five fours and two sixes would have been outstanding in any circumstances but to produce that performance at that time was the stuff of dreams, and for him to win two man-of-the-match awards in a single day simply underlined that!

Amidst the post-match mayhem, I suffered an accidental elbow to the nose as I jumped up in celebration of the winning runs but soon dismissed the pain as Mo gathered the boys for a quick huddle. He very briefly reinforced the messages he had previously conveyed, telling us that we had won because we deserved to win and choosing that unforgettable moment to further instil belief in the young players about their ability and what they were capable of in the future. Publicly, he rightly drew attention to the part played in the triumph by Bumpy who, he said, 'brought these guys up'. For his own part he commented that he had always been 'calm inside' and believed strongly that we would win. That, of course, was exactly what he had told the group, and it is no coincidence that in their media interviews both Barny and Coxy cited the skipper's reassuring, positive influence as a major element in our collective success.

It is not difficult to imagine the scenes in the dressing room after the game. There was champagne, singing and general pandemonium. My family came in for a few minutes and, not surprisingly, a couple of the Bretforton boys managed to gain access! I'm pleased that I was able, an hour or so later, to escape the chaos for a few minutes and to take it all in. I slipped out on to the Edgbaston dressing room balcony and sat, beer in hand, surveying the almost empty stadium illuminated then by just a few spotlights and not the glaring floodlights of earlier.

Rather like when I reflected, on a different balcony some three years later, on the entirety of my career, I can't be specific about my musings at the end of that long day, but chief amongst them, I'm sure, was pride. Two years earlier, at the lowest point of my professional life, I had made a choice to stay with Worcestershire when, had I let emotion govern my judgement, I might have decided otherwise. Now I felt beyond any iota of doubt that I had done the right thing. To have been part of one of the greatest days in the club's history was genuinely moving, and all those old cliches about this being a reward for the hours, days, months and years of effort and sacrifice made by myself and other family members, were somewhere in my mind. There can be few comparable feelings as a sportsman to sitting after a victory, physically and mentally spent but emotionally euphoric.

To have won a County Championship would arguably have been a greater achievement but even that would never have provided one single day which could match what we had just experienced. Apart from international cricket, there is no other scenario which could have compared to that occasion. With the widespread media coverage, playing in front of a crowd of something like 25,000 and the general exhilaration of the whole experience, the day was not just unforgettable but deeply meaningful. It is difficult to express in words, but I honestly felt that my entire Worcestershire cricket existence had somehow been justified by that one triumph. The fact that I had waited so long and that we had suffered so many disappointments in the late stages of previous one-day competitions made it all the sweeter.

With the following summer disturbed by flooding at New Road which necessitated us playing two home Championship games at Kidderminster in mid-season, 2019 saw us disappoint badly in the red-ball game. Despite going into the season feeling confident that we could mount a serious promotion challenge and winning the first two fixtures, we won only once more and finished second from bottom of Division Two. A return of 559 runs represented one of my least productive first-class seasons and the fact that two hundreds were included in that tally indicates the general mediocrity of my form. In the white-ball stuff, however, we were once again impressive, and reached the quarter-finals of the 50-over tournament after narrowly finishing second to Nottinghamshire in the North Group, only to be well-beaten at home by Somerset. I batted at No.4 throughout and even made a century in the first game at Old Trafford as well as contributing significantly with the ball in most games, but it was once again the Twenty20 Blast that probably defined our season.

I was left out of the side for the first match, a win at Trent Bridge but subsequently played in every game as we finished fourth in our group to set up an away quarter-final against Sussex at Hove, an affair settled by one of the most stunning exhibitions of limited-overs batting I have ever witnessed. Chasing 185 to win, we charged home with more than two overs to spare as Moeen hammered an unbeaten 121 off just 60 balls and hit 11 sixes. I have to confess that, in an attempt to assuage my nerves, I watched our innings on the television in the dressing room and only emerged to join the celebrations as the teams left the field. That was something of a bizarre experience in itself, since the short delay between live events and the transmitted pictures meant that the sounds from outside generally conveyed when something exciting had happened, but, being inside, I was never exactly sure what!

After waiting so long for our first finals day we were off to Edgbaston again and confident that we could repeat the success of our previous visit. Despite making only occasional minor contributions with the bat, I absolutely relished my role in the side that year as a bowler, and probably produced the most consistent form in that discipline in any season of my career.

My economy rate of 6.41 in sending down a total of 36 overs was, I hope, a key factor in our success and certainly made me feel that I was still a valuable member of the group. It was particularly satisfying to believe that aspects of my performance were still improving, even at that late stage in my career.

My bowling in Twenty20 cricket was still growing in its effectiveness as I gained experience. I am certain that being primarily a batter helped in that regard, since it made it easier to figure out what an opponent might be thinking at any point, to assess where they might be aiming to score for example and coming up with an approach to negate that. I definitely developed more effective strategies in bowling at left-handers and the fact that my bowling lacked pace made it more difficult for batters we term '360 degree' players, those capable of hitting big shots behind square on both sides of the wicket, to hit me for that kind of boundary shot. In summary, my approach was to make it possible to hit me for six only by clearing a fielder.

Almost inevitably, our second finals day failed to match the marvellous climax of the first, even though it came very close and involved its own astonishing moments of excitement. Grabbing victory in the semi-final against Notts when they needed just seven off Wayne Parnell's last over, and one off the final ball, was almost beyond belief. This was a thought which must have been shared by their skipper, Dan Christian, who, having been caught in the ring off Pat in the penultimate over of the innings reacted to Browny's perhaps over-enthusiastic celebration in combative mood. I was in close proximity as he strolled off uttering the words 'Calm down, mate. We only need f***ing ten!' As we left the field following the climax, I put my arm around Pat's shoulder and suggested he might want to let DC know they had only managed eight!

On the other side of the coin, Ravi Bopara's brilliance and Simon Harmer's successive fours off the last two balls of the 20th over of the Essex innings in the final itself, broke our collective hearts as a second consecutive Blast title was snatched away. Harmer had won two man-of-the-match awards in one day, proving, exactly as Ben Cox had done 12 months before, that when a top cricketer has their day and the cricketing gods are smiling upon them everybody else simply has to live with it.

The crushing disappointment of losing off the last ball in such dramatic circumstances has, of course, to be regarded as the defining emotion of the whole event, but it's also my belief that, in some respects, it was an even better experience than the previous year. Certainly, the thrilling unpredictability of the cricket, and the emotional roller-coaster ride, was a match for anything I have ever encountered in sport, and once the aching rawness of defeat had slightly eased, I was able to appreciate just how enjoyable it had been. Nonetheless, I spent most of the evening sitting bolt upright staring into space and I suspect I wasn't the only Worcestershire player who couldn't sleep that night.

For every winner, there's a loser and it's obvious that sportsmen and women throughout history have had to cope with defeat, recover and get on with life. It might be an utterly unimaginative cliche but cricket actually is only a game and a few short months later events beyond anybody's control brought about changes to our lives which were to have far-reaching consequences not only for the rest of my playing career but for the world in general.

13

NEW CHALLENGES

IN JANUARY 2020, as everybody will remember, we first heard of coronavirus, but in the first month or two of the year nobody was really aware of the impact it would have on our lives. There were some highly knowledgeable epidemiologists who had an inkling of its potential severity, but most of us, I suppose, hoped that it would result in a fairly brief disruption to the routines of our daily lives. As the pandemic developed, however, it soon became clear that things were considerably more serious than anybody had anticipated. As chair of the PCA, I found myself heavily involved in the coordination of county cricket's response to the unprecedented situation.

My work with the PCA had begun back in 2009 when I became the Worcestershire representative on the association's committee. That was a reasonably straightforward role which involved attending occasional meetings, passing on information to my county colleagues and generally ensuring that their voices were heard in any significant debates which demanded player input. I was also the first port of call for any of my team-mates if they had an issue regarding their professional lives in any respect. Becoming chair of the Players' Committee, comprised of all the 18 county representatives and the England women's representative, in February 2017 had obviously increased the workload and the commitment required to successfully fulfil the position. In terms of the constitution of the PCA, that committee is effectively all-powerful, though the daily running of the organisation is delegated to the executive board which, of course, includes the chair.

By far the single most important aspect of my work with the association in my first two years as chair was my input into the creation of the County Partnership Agreement (CPA) between the ECB and the cricket network. Started in November 2017, the PCA set out several non-negotiable principles regarding the remuneration of players. The ECB had just landed a £1.1 bn television deal and the PCA was simply trying to ensure that the players received their fair share of the money.

Cricket might, as I mentioned earlier, be only a game but at professional level almost all its players are entirely dependent upon it for their income. It is a short career for most, and the protection of their rights is the association's fundamental responsibility. Essentially, we agreed that the players would receive a minimum of 26.5% of the ECB's annual revenue, were guaranteed a binding minimum wage and implemented a new 'rookie contract', geared towards 18- to 21-year-olds who were starting out in the professional game. The agreement also dealt with some quite intricate detail around remuneration to be paid to players selected for The Hundred, contract dates, injury insurance, freedom of player movement in the winter months, the funding of the England men's and women's teams, financing of the women's game in general, and fairer HR procedures.

Another vital component of our plan as an association was the establishment of the Futures Fund, an initiative to aid the transition of members at the end of their playing careers into the next stages of their working lives. It was settled that all counties would pay 3% of their Team Salary Payment into the fund every year with the money managed by a trust set up by the PCA. We had demonstrated, after studying all available data, that players leaving the game, particularly between the ages of 28 and 32, had experienced considerable difficulty in moving into alternative employment and the thinking behind the scheme was to help them in that transition. Basically, the longer their service to the game, the more they stood to benefit.

This five-year deal, running from January 2020 to the end of 2024, was the result of almost two years, and countless hours, of travelling, discussion, planning and negotiation. I played a leading part in the process, helping to devise the detail, liaising with county representatives to ensure that all parties felt that their interests were being considered, and generally facilitating the delivery of what was a landmark agreement. It was a time-consuming and demanding achievement but one which was ultimately hugely satisfying. I had been entrusted by my fellow players with the responsibility of safeguarding their livelihoods and I was proud to consider that I, as part of the team, had delivered. In terms of my own professional development, I had taken several giant steps forward, too, and garnered experience and skills which I was certain would benefit me in the future. All this had been achieved while I was still playing, of course, and against the backdrop of the on-field success we as a club had enjoyed in 2018 and 2019.

The Hundred, a completely new and revolutionary form of the game, was actually under development during that same period. As early as September 2016 the ECB had been considering a new city-based Twenty20 tournament, a rival to the Indian Premier League, and in April 2017, following discussions with the counties, the PCA and the MCC, it was decided to pursue this option. Then, later that year, Sanjay Patel, the ECB's chief commercial officer at the time, came up with the idea of creating a totally novel, 100-ball version of cricket. His initial vision was sufficiently supported and further shaped, to the point that the ECB called Matthew Wheeler, then the non-executive chair of the PCA board, and me to a specially arranged meeting at Lord's at the very start of the 2018 season.

We were shown a colourful and upbeat promotional video which ended with the big reveal that this new version of cricket was to be called The Hundred. I must admit that at first, I didn't really 'get it' but Matthew was more enthusiastic. My first thoughts were that the creation of a new format was to protect the Twenty20 Blast owing to a belief that there wasn't room for two separate 20-over competitions.

There might be some truth in suggestions that a new game, based on 100 balls, without overs but with sets of five balls and a change of ends after every ten, might be easier to understand and thus attract a new cricket audience, but that did not particularly occur to me at the time. At that point we were both sworn to secrecy as the county CEOs had not been consulted, though by 19 April, the eve of our second County Championship game of that 2018 season, which was at Taunton, the concept had been approved and announced to the public.

Returning to our hotel after practice that afternoon I found myself bombarded by dozens of text messages, emails and phone calls from players up and down the land asking just what on earth was going on! From mid-afternoon until late at night, I was occupied with the task of explaining the potential implications of the new venture, intended to start in 2020, to concerned PCA members.

I had been re-elected as chair in early 2019 and was happy to continue, since at that point I felt that a number of initiatives, including the actual delivery of the CPA, were ongoing and there were still jobs to complete. Then, with the new deal actually up and running but very much in its infancy, my next, and completely unexpected, challenge came as I was required to manage the players' part in the domestic game's response to the pandemic.

With the UK in lockdown from late March it quickly became apparent that the 2020 season would not go ahead as scheduled. In the same month England's tour of Sri Lanka was abandoned and the players flew home, then the ECB announced that the season would not start as planned on 12 April but would be delayed until at least the end of May. On 24 April a further statement was issued saying that there would certainly be no cricket until July, and a few days later came the decision that the launch of the new 100-ball venture would be pushed back to 2021.

By this point the government job retention (furlough) scheme had been introduced and it clearly fell to me to coordinate any potential inclusion of the players in the programme. Not surprisingly my PCA members, many of whom had families and financial commitments to consider, just like members of other professions all over the United Kingdom, were seriously concerned about how they would cope. Following a considerable number of online group meetings and lengthy private conversations with various county reps, and especially with James Harris and Heather Knight, my two deputies, it was my duty to come up with an effective strategy to make the financial outcomes workable both for my members and for the counties, several of which were already operating within extremely tight budgetary restrictions.

Undoubtedly that was the greatest challenge I had ever faced in my time at the PCA to that point. I was constantly aware that my decisions would directly impact upon the daily lives not only of the players who had elected me, but also on their partners and families. One of the especially important considerations was the absolute necessity to safeguard those in the final year of their contracts at such an uncertain time.

On average 45 county cricketers retire or are released every year and going into the 2020 season we, as a players' committee, knew that well over 100 colleagues were in the last year of their current agreements, so we envisaged a potential mass exodus from the professional game, and therefore had to plan for that. Our solution was that any players who were eventually released at the end of that season got a full refund of any salary reduction which had been applied to them. Such players would also benefit from the immediate implementation of the aforementioned Futures Fund and a new standard contract, one of the benefits of which was two months' contract expiry payments. All of which was funded in one year by players relinquishing their prize money.

Whilst to some it might have appeared that we were trying to force through pay cuts, what we were really striving to do was maintain jobs and protect our most vulnerable members. It was the first time that I had ever been involved in negotiations which were not universally seen as positive; in almost all contexts, the PCA work which I had undertaken so far was to ensure outcomes whereby everyone was gaining something. This could be viewed differently. I was basically approving the removal of sizeable chunks of salary from my friends and colleagues, not just at New Road but up and down the country. It did not sit easy with me and I had to endure more than a few sleepless nights and very many difficult conversations. The maturity and conscientiousness which the county reps showed in that process was admirable and the final outcome was an acceptable and sensible compromise. We certainly played our part in keeping counties alive!

Eventually the players agreed to cuts in salary which, along with the relinquishment of any prize money which would otherwise have been paid, saved the professional game £3.8 million. Being on fixed-term contracts with no lay-off clauses in place, the playing members of the PCA actually volunteered to accept being furloughed and thus the counties benefited by a further £4 million.

The ingenious creation of bio-secure bubbles, using grounds which had on-site hotel facilities, allowed some international cricket to be played from midsummer, but to all intents and purposes the season was decimated. The cancellation of The Hundred and the hugely curtailed men's and women's domestic competitions, which didn't eventually begin until August, meant, of course, that it was pretty much a write-off season in financial terms and we at the PCA felt a responsibility to assist the game in so far as we could. On 9 September, as we approached the end of a severely truncated season, I issued an official PCA press release in which I attempted to explain fully the efforts my members had made. It ran as follows:

As we enter the final stages of the most challenging summer of our careers, it is important to reflect and appreciate how the game of cricket and players in particular have worked together over the course of the last six months to protect current and future careers.

With 134 men's county players out of contract when the season was due to begin in April and the game set to welcome 40 new professionals in the women's game, it meant a large percentage of our playing membership were fearing for their jobs. Despite all of this, players approached the challenge with understanding and the voluntary financial losses for players in 2020 reflect this.

International and domestic players supported the game through volunteering in the region of £3.8 million. When other losses such as the cancellation of The Hundred, delayed contracts for the new women's domestic structure and consent to furlough are taken into account, the game has saved in the region of £15m since April thanks to player support.

With the support of my vice-chairs, Heather Knight and James Harris, as well as the players' committee I believe the current playing group have shown a great responsibility to protect each other and future players.

The protracted nature of the preparatory work required to bring about the CPA, and the occurrence of Covid-19 with the issues it created for the game, meant that I had become chair of the PCA in just about the worst period imaginable in terms of the time demands of the job. On the opposite side of that argument, however, I had been presented with opportunities to demonstrate my capability in an administrative position and this undoubtedly contributed to the decision made by the board to offer me the director of cricket operations position which I eventually assumed.

Sitting on one committee or another in a meeting at ECB headquarters at Lord's, or in the PCA offices at The Oval, became commonplace for me throughout my period as chair and eventually became just another aspect of my professional life. It seemed as if I spent as many days on the train to London, or staying in a hotel in the capital as I did playing or training, and I must have become a familiar figure to other commuters to the capital from Worcester.

Learning to switch between roles, to move from player to administrator from one day to the next, often even having to make that switch within the same day, was difficult at first but became easier as I grew into the job, until eventually tapping away on the laptop was almost as routine as playing a forward defensive. Indeed, from 2017 onwards I would often find a quiet space in whatever ground we might be playing at to hide myself away and get some administrative work done when my presence was not required elsewhere. I am certain that had no negative impact whatever on my cricket and might even have been a positive factor. Although there are some well-documented stories of high-profile players whose apparent obsession with cricket drives their top-level performances, I always found that ability to switch off and change focus genuinely beneficial when it came to managing my own game.

I have long believed that most professional cricketers perform better on the field if their lives are enhanced by wider interests and activities, and that is an attitude which I have consistently attempted to foster in my PCA members. An increasing focus on player education, developing work experience opportunities and generally encouraging breadth of interest, is at the heart of the association's work. Not only does this help to improve the prospects of its members when their playing days are over but, in most cases I think, a broader outlook on life, not solely cricket driven, provides a stabilising backdrop against which to perform. This makes players more likely to handle success and failure with a level mindset, thus protecting their mental health.

Personnel changes at board level at the PCA, which were caused by a variety of factors, meant that throughout the period my own involvement in planning, decision-making and implementation of several key projects was actually one of the few constants.

On various high-profile occasions I found myself standing in front of hundreds of people, often including many of my county colleagues in the Long Room or at some similar hallowed venue, addressing an audience of cricket dignitaries, many of whose profiles far exceed my own in terms of fame and influence. What were originally quite nerve-racking occasions became fairly commonplace and though I never took such commitments lightly, over time they grew to be less daunting. At first, I did occasionally wonder how the boy from Bret had come to find himself in such esteemed company but, in keeping with my general character, I tended to deal with each situation as it arose and was able to find a way to manage the demands with which I was faced. At all times, I was driven to a large extent by the realisation that my position was dictated by the faith that my fellow professionals had placed in me to represent their interests.

County cricket eventually did get underway in August when a new competition, the Bob Willis Trophy, began. Willis, the former Surrey and Warwickshire fast bowler who gained legendary status as an England hero following his Ashes exploits in 1981 and went on to become a pillar of TV cricket punditry, had died in December 2019 and the idea of a red-ball tournament in his honour, to replace the County Championship for that one Covid-hit year was an imaginative solution to the problem faced by the domestic first-class game. The 18 counties were split into three regional groups to minimise travelling and each team would play each other just once before the two group winners with the most points advanced to a Lord's final.

Following months of isolation, and to all intents and purposes without any real preparation, players across the country returned to action in empty grounds, yet the competition was a success in many respects. The general mood was one of relief mixed with joy; the lack of spectators and a hugely different set of circumstances regarding changing and catering facilities on all grounds did little to quell the positive feelings of most players. Gymnasiums, dining rooms and hospitality suites were transformed into changing rooms and the collective desire to get out and play was shared by most. It was a pleasant reminder, I think, for many cricketers of just why we play the game. We forgot for a moment the money, the prizes and the media spotlight and remembered that we just enjoyed playing cricket!

Our season began at Bristol and once we had adjusted to the practices necessary to adhere to pandemic protocols it was back to business. The ground, like every other, was separated into different zones, whose access was limited to particular groups, and there were plenty of stewards on hand to remind everybody where they could or couldn't go. On the field we quickly became familiar with such things as sanitisation breaks after every six overs which allowed players and officials to clean their hands and the ball, reserves who carried items on and off the playing area wore gloves and so on. In retrospect, it seems we managed well enough and, of course, we will never really know whether or not such practices, which eventually continued into the next season, were truly effective, but at least we were playing.

Any sportsman who has gone out to play undercooked, meaning without having had the opportunity to prepare fully for their performance, often fears the worst only to find that, just sometimes, their experience and instincts mean that they manage to produce decent form. Many a golfer, for sure, has played a fine round despite not having picked up a club for a few weeks. It's not necessarily that common but it does happen. In this case the nation's cricketers were at least all in the same boat; the batters hadn't hit many balls but nor had the bowlers delivered many, so perhaps things evened themselves out. In any event the matches produced some exciting, meaningful cricket and were widely enjoyed. An often-overlooked consequence of the situation was the significant development of counties' streaming services with games being offered via a variety of online platforms thus allowing supporters to follow their progress. The improvement in this area, which has since continued, might well in years to come be regarded as an unexpected bonus of the decision to push ahead with some sort of programme in that most difficult of years.

Alex Gidman had taken over as head coach when Sharpy decided to take a slightly less prominent role as head of coach and player development late in 2018. His preparations had primarily been aimed at red-ball cricket. In particular Alex made it clear that we must become harder to beat in the four-day game. Judged alongside that ambition our Bob Willis Trophy campaign was definitely successful, since we won two, drew two and lost only one of our five fixtures. Since that solitary defeat came in the last game, against the eventual group winners, Somerset, at New Road, we did not qualify for the final but certainly played some solid and meaningful cricket.

My own form was pleasing, as I made 80 in the very first innings of the tournament, 94 in the second innings of the next game and then a hundred in a drawn home game at Warwickshire, a particularly important innings for me since it was my maiden first-class century against our local rivals. Though I averaged over 40, on reflection I feel that I missed out slightly as on both of those other occasions when I had passed 50 I got myself out when well set. As an opening batsman it was oddly refreshing to start four-day cricket in August when weather and pitch conditions tend to favour the batter.

Arguably, the most enjoyable moment of the whole season from a team point of view came in the win at Northampton, when Tom Fell made a century, his first in first-class cricket since his career-best 171 against Middlesex in the last game of the 2015 season. Shortly after that game Felly had been diagnosed with testicular cancer and missed a considerable part of the next year's cricket. The fact that it was a match-winning knock made it special enough, but viewed as a victory over adversity, a long-awaited milestone passed in a personal battle that had encompassed chemotherapy, and then a frustrating few years when that elusive three-figure score just would not come, it becomes immensely significant. I know he felt as though a massive burden had been lifted from his shoulders and it was an emotional moment for us all. There were few, if any, spectators at Wantage Road that day but those of us that were present made as much noise as we possibly could when he passed three figures.

The points that I have already made about the difficulty of achieving high standards of performance in both red- and white-ball cricket at the same time were possibly more apt that season, since the only other competition which took place was the Twenty20 Blast. Therefore, it is perhaps no surprise that alongside our improvement in the four-day stuff we did not match the levels of the previous two seasons in the shorter format. Lacking key contributors like Wayne Parnell and Mo meant that we were not as competitive as before, especially with the ball, and we won only two of our games, played in the same geographical group as in the Bob Willis Trophy.

Pandemic restrictions were still in place when what would prove to be my final season began, and a revised structure had been agreed the previous October, for one year only, to mitigate their impact. Teams were split into three divisions and the opening rounds were, as in the previous year, played behind closed doors but some crowds were admitted later on. Borrowing the idea, though not the exact configurations, of three groups of six from the Bob Willis Trophy experience of 2020, the new arrangements proved reasonably if not universally popular and, as we now know, a return to the traditional two-division Championship was agreed for 2022.

I have previously mentioned our mediocre collective performance in 2021 and, apart from a couple of highlights, for me personally it was not a season to remember with great fondness. One was my last century, albeit in something of a dead rubber draw against Warwickshire at New Road, and the other came in a game at Derby in July when I dismissed Leus du Plooy to become the first Worcestershire bowler to take 100 wickets in Twenty20 cricket. The 50-over competition was generally regarded as a development opportunity and Worcestershire, like many other counties, fielded relatively inexperienced teams. This meant that I played no part, and since I was also left out of the Twenty20 side on various occasions my closing season turned out to be, in truth, somewhat anticlimactic.

14

PICK OF THE PEARS

IT WAS my privilege and pleasure to play for Worcestershire with many great cricketers across the years. Our overseas recruits included a string of outstanding names and most impressed both on and off the pitch, though one or two, like Shoaib Akhtar, didn't necessarily reserve their best performances for the Pears. Shoaib was signed by Tom Moody to play the second half of the 2005 season but by the time of his arrival in Worcester, our coach had left to join Sri Lanka, and thus 'The Rawalpindi Express', as he was widely known, wasn't exactly on track!

Shoaib was part cricketer, part rock star and his chosen form of transport during his stay with us was a Harley-Davidson motorcycle. In 2002, he had become the first bowler ever to be recorded bowling at 100mph, and from that day forward, had commanded a certain amount of awe in most cricket circles. Unfortunately, however, the lads in the dressing room were far more concerned with him producing the goods in matches rather than how impressive his historical exploits or off-field image were, and he rarely did the business in a Worcestershire shirt.

Like many such luminaries, Shoaib had a constant companion, a sort of valet or personal assistant, who attended to his needs on a routine basis. I remember one particularly amusing incident concerning his aide. Following a disappointing effort in the field in a Twenty20 game, Vikram, the captain at the time, was treating us to one of his quite rare bollockings, and leaving nobody in any doubt as to their shortcomings. Suddenly, he was interrupted by a knock on the door. Shoaib's pal walked in to deliver a burger and chips to his boss! The great man then proceeded to devour his meal mid-bollocking, as the rest of us struggled to contain our giggles!

Apart from an especially memorable, almost single-handed, destruction of Gloucestershire in a one-day game at New Road, when he bowled at express pace to grab a match-winning 6-16 in just seven overs, having been called in as a reluctant, and therefore angry, replacement for an injured Gareth Batty, there were few highlights. A couple of seriously rapid spells in Championship cricket really served only to emphasise what we were missing most of the time.

An exhaustive list of our overseas visitors would reveal a star-studded array of talent and, if I am completely honest, I have to say that the many names, Ravi Ashwin, Shannon Gabriel, Dilhara Fernando, Doug Bollinger, Lou Vincent, Abdul Razzaq, Andy Bichel, Alzarri Joseph, Mitchell Santner and Thilan Samaraweera to name but ten hardly previously mentioned, do fade into the mists of time. Likewise, some of the dozens of players with whom I have gone into battle over the years are difficult to recall, and that isn't at all to tarnish their efforts in any way.

While I wouldn't say that I was an avid student of Worcestershire cricket history, I always tried to have a respect for the club's past and an awareness of some of its great names from before my own time as a player. Many people trot out those quotations about the past informing the future, and, as with a lot of cliches, there's some truth in that idea. 'If you don't know where you come from, you don't know where you're going' is the sort of thing I have in mind. Of course, it's perfectly possible for a player to play brilliantly for any team without knowing anything substantial about its past and especially if he's a brief visitor, an overseas player, say, or even, in modern times, a loanee perhaps.

I have always thought any regular member of a county team ought to have some knowledge of, and respect for, those who have preceded them. In order to properly appreciate your own position, it's probably fair to say that you need to understand the feelings and thoughts of supporters and members, too. If you are part of a team which is pushing for honours in a particular competition, knowing your county's history, its previous success or lack of it, is obviously informative. How long has the club and its followers waited for possible success? When was the last time it won something significant? And if you become, as I did, captain, and an almost permanent fixture in a county set-up for almost two decades, it's only natural that you begin to see yourself as relevant in that history. That carries with it, I hope, no sense of arrogance on my behalf, no suggestion that I qualify for any particular status other than that of a player who through sheer long service made himself part of the Worcestershire story.

It is a favourite pastime of county followers to choose their all-time best team and things are no different where the Pears are concerned. It's notoriously difficult to compare players from different eras, of course, and so I generally tend to confine my personal observations to those with whom I actually performed. Nonetheless, I am completely aware of some of the wonderful cricketers who represented Worcestershire before I came along, and have been fortunate and grateful to have met more than a few.

Clearly I am unable fully to appraise the relative quality of those from the dim and distant past and, like everybody else in the current era, I have to rely on scorecards and the written word generally, to formulate my opinions regarding the likes of Ted Arnold, the seven (!) Foster brothers, Fred Root, Reg Perks, Peter Jackson, Sid Martin, Dick Howorth, 'Doc' Gibbons, the Nawab of Pataudi and the like. I have spoken to members who actually saw some of the slightly later greats, like Roly Jenkins and the Richardson brothers, Peter and Dick, and many who remember the exploits of the fine teams of the 1960s containing greats like Don Kenyon, Martin Horton, Ron Headley, Roy Booth, Basil D'Oliveira, Norman Gifford, Alan Ormrod, Jack Flavell, Len Coldwell and Tom Graveney. I stress that this is not intended to be an exhaustive list and hope I will be forgiven if I have failed to mention some important names!

Frequent meetings with Tom, Martin, Roy, Basil, Norman and others from that period were always pleasurable for me and reminded me of the fact that my own part in the club's story, like theirs, was just a transitory one. Similarly, my conversations over the years with the great Glenn Turner and his contemporaries, with Vanburn Holder and with Duncan Fearnley, who was the club chairman during the successful period in the late 80s, helped me understand my own place in the bigger picture. In the final few seasons of my career, the dedication of another of those stalwarts, Paul Pridgeon, in his role as chair of the Cricket Steering Group, was an unwavering reminder of just how big a part of someone's life a commitment to Worcestershire can become.

When it comes to the outstanding years of the late 80s and early 90s, my appreciation is more tangible, since many of the key performers are still quite familiar figures whom I know well or, in some cases, saw in action. Playing alongside Hicky, working with Bumpy and Pridge, regularly conversing with Phil Neale, Tim Curtis, Neal Radford, Richard Illingworth and others, helped me to understand my own responsibilities, first as a player and later as a captain.

I have often been asked to select the best Worcestershire team from those with whom I played and have found it an enjoyable and thought-provoking exercise. After some consideration, I have decided that in recognition of the way the game has moved on in terms of specialisation, the only sensible way to approach the challenge is to pick a team to play red-ball cricket and another for the white-ball game. So here goes.

There are five players who make both sides, and umpteen who might consider themselves hard done by to miss out, but it is, after all, a light-hearted and patently subjective exercise. I hope that means I will be excused for naming myself in one of the line-ups when I know there are probably lots of more appealing candidates. I freely admit that a number of my selections are based simply on personal preference, and are not necessarily entirely justifiable when statistics are examined in detail. And inevitably I am envisaging players performing as they did when at their very best for the Pears, or at least how I remember them at a particular time.

Red-ball team

1. Daryl Mitchell

I am taking the liberty of including myself in the chosen XI for the longer game. There have, as I have already intimated, been more talented and watchable opening batsmen than me, but I claim that my consistency and longevity justify my selection. I'm also offering the side a decent pair of hands in the slip cordon and the option of some occasional 'pies' with the ball. In the first-class game I might have managed only 33 wickets but I was able on many occasions to restrict the scoring rate, mainly because batsmen feared the embarrassment of getting out to my innocuous offerings!

2. Phillip Hughes

To go in with me at the top of the order I am choosing Phillip Hughes. This is one selection which is partly governed by an emotional bias, jointly forged by my personal relationship with the player and by the tragic nature of his passing. Phil actually only played nine first-class games for us, made two hundreds and averaged a solid but unspectacular 35, but even in those few appearances created a huge impression. Walking out to the middle at the start of an innings is considerably easier if you have complete trust in your partner and that's how I always felt with Hughesy. Such trust is not confined to calling and running between the wickets as some might imagine, but includes shared opinions on conditions, bowlers, match situations and opposition field settings. Valued input from the other end can sometimes be useful in making assessments about your own game, too, so being out there with someone with whom you share a mutual understanding is especially helpful.

3. Graeme Hick

There won't be many who disagree with this pick. Graeme Hick would surely nail down the No.3 spot in any Worcestershire XI, even if it were picked from all those who have represented the club since its very beginning, not just those with whom I played. I have already eulogised about his many qualities and would simply add that his consistency of performance and, importantly, of behaviour was additionally remarkable. Having a player in your side who almost never fails to deliver, who always stands up when it matters and simply never shirks a contest is a captain's dream, and that player was Hicky.

4. Vikram Solanki (captain)

At No.4, I choose as captain another of the major influences on me in every regard, the complete gentleman that is Vikram Solanki. In many respects, his career was similar to my own numerically – he played well over 200 times for the Pears and made 29 centuries at an average of 35.36 before his departure – and like me, he also led the side with distinction for a number of years. His style, general composure and overall impact on the playing side of things during those seasons was immeasurable and I cannot imagine excluding him. My trust in his judgement and tactical appreciation make him the obvious choice to lead my imaginary team.

5. Joe Clarke

Next comes Joe Clarke, in some eyes a slightly contentious figure whose progress in the game following a pretty explosive introduction has been hampered by off-field controversy. In this context, I am concerning myself only with cricket. As soon as Joe came into the senior environment at New Road, he impressed me and eventually I liked what he brought. He immediately set about imposing his character on the side and my initial impression, partly shaped by my own memories of how tentatively I had made my first steps into the professional game, was of a rather cocky, possibly slightly arrogant young man. However, I quickly changed my mindset and gained huge respect for him when it became clear that he worked extremely hard at his game and his confidence was backed up by performance, and I mean consistently not just occasionally. It's probably fair to say that from an early stage Joe considered himself the best player in the team and he probably was.

Joe played only 55 times at first-class level before leaving us for Trent Bridge but in that time, he scored over 3,500 runs, made 12 centuries and averaged comfortably over 40. Not bad for a youngster! Throw in his blistering capabilities in the white-ball game and you realise that he is a very fine player. At the time of writing, success in franchise cricket has propelled him into the short format spotlight, but it has been my feeling right from the very beginning of his career that Joe has what it takes to excel at the highest level in the longer game. He has demonstrated that he can play all around the wicket and has the very rare ability to score runs, even boundaries, off really good deliveries from seriously good bowlers. He knows it, too, and as long as that self-belief remains on the right side of the line between confidence and arrogance, he is capable of achieving special things in the game.

6. Moeen Ali

Mo is an easy selection. To have within the ranks a genuine all-rounder capable of match-winning performances with both bat and ball is priceless, and his ability to galvanise those around him is an added bonus. One of the criteria that I have applied in making my selections is the likely contribution of team members to the sort of positive collective mood which brings success, and in Mo's case that is guaranteed.

7. Steven Davies

At No.7, I include my wicketkeeper, Steven Davies. One of my oldest friends in the game, since we started together in age group sides in our early teens, Davo is perhaps not the very best gloveman with whom I've ever played but is nonetheless a fine technician behind the stumps. As a batter, though, he offers a variety of skills. He is possessed of a sound understanding of his strengths and can score runs quickly when necessary whilst at the same time being able to dig in and battle when conditions are difficult. In his time at New Road, he averaged 36.88 in first-class cricket and that return is more than satisfactory as far as I'm concerned.

8. Zaheer Khan

It's always good to have variety in a seam bowling attack and a high-class left-arm swing bowler is a great asset. It was relatively early in my career when Zaheer Khan made his 16 first-class appearances for us but he left a lasting impression upon me owing to his tremendous versatility. He had complete mastery of the range of skills which pacemen can offer. He could swing the ball both ways, reverse it, gain sideways movement in either direction off the pitch and produce yorkers at will, while also being capable of delivering some really quick spells.

At the time he was with us, in 2006, he was desperate to regain his place in the Indian Test set-up and consequently was a seriously driven individual with a remarkable desire to bowl as many overs as possible. His 9-138 against Essex at Chelmsford is one of the all-time best returns for a Worcestershire bowler and 78 wickets in his brief stint with us tells its own story. What I especially remember is Zaheer's uncanny ability to recognise what was likely to be the best approach in any given conditions; it seemed that within a couple of overs, he was able to assess a pitch and to then adopt whatever method was necessary to maximise his effectiveness.

9. Saeed Ajmal

No.9 might be slightly too high in the batting order for Saeed but that's a risk I'm willing to take in order to accommodate the breadth of talent my fantasy team encompasses. Prior to

PICK OF THE PEARS

being forced to remodel his action owing to questions being raised regarding its legitimacy, he was simply magnificent for us.

The difficulty of making judgements about such technical aspects of a biomechanical nature means that there will always be those who dispute various evaluations of the quality of performance of certain bowlers but I am basing my selection simply on what I witnessed from Saeed, largely in 2014. His control of line and length was immaculate and the rare ability to turn the ball both ways thanks to his doosra made him a match-winner. Knowing that we had his bowling to depend on inspired confidence in the batting group and his 63 wickets at just 16.48 runs each in that season were instrumental in our success. A warm and generous personality, Saeed was always a pleasure to play alongside.

10. Simon Jones

It's a great pity that we didn't see more of Simon at New Road. In fact, he played only nine times for us in the first-class game but still managed to grab 42 wickets in that 2008 promotion campaign. Who knows what his eventual career numbers might have looked like had he not been so plagued by injury? He had the quintessential fast bowler's personality. Indeed, I don't think I ever encountered a more aggressive bowler than Simon, who just hated batsmen in whatever situation, and that included net practice. He possessed true pace but was also tremendously skilful, and in particular a master of reverse swing. His sheer strength was impressive, too, and I well remember that at one stage whilst recovering from injury, he bowled at us in practice off just two or three paces but was still comfortably the quickest bowler in our ranks. Jonesy rarely resorted to any kind of verbal attack when bowling, relying instead on a chilling stare and the utter potency of his deliveries. He was absolutely the sort of character you want in your camp.

11. Alan Richardson

Every side needs a workhorse, a bowler to whom a captain can throw the ball at any point in a game and pretty much know what he's going to get. For me, Richo was that guy during the four-year spell that he spent in the first team at Worcestershire. I have already detailed his qualities as a player and as a mentor of others, but it is the absolute dependability of the man that most characterises him, and that is what gets him the nod ahead of several other candidates. Richo happily shares a story about a message he received from Graeme Hick when he passed 1,000 career runs in 2012. It read 'Congratulations on achieving 1,000 runs in your 30-year career. Some of us manage to do it in

30 days!' It actually took Alan only 18 years, but you get the idea.

12. Joe Leach

I have to include Joe as 12th man, partly to ease my conscience because he absolutely deserves to be more than just one of the many names I've overlooked. His 360 first-class wickets for the Pears in the years up to my retirement have cost only 24.65 runs each and speak of his qualities. As a new-ball bowler, there have been few better in county cricket in that time and his skiddy style has been especially suited to bowling at New Road where pitches have tended not to offer a huge amount of bounce. Joe is someone who attacks the stumps and thus makes the batsman play most of the time. He picks up a lot of his wickets either bowled or lbw but also threatens both edges of the bat with his seam movement. He is also a well above average lower-middle-order batter and an intelligent cricketer who has undoubtedly made the most of his abilities.

White ball team

1. Vikram Solanki

All I would add to my comments about Vikram's qualities as outlined above, is that in the shorter formats he could absolutely dismantle opposition bowling attacks whilst all the time playing what I might term proper cricket shots. Though perfectly capable of making runs via innovative and unorthodox methods, generally he was able to score quickly without taking the unnecessary risks associated with such an approach. The result was that he tended to go about his business at the top of the order in one-day cricket still focused on building his innings properly rather than just trying to blast his way to a score from ball one.

2. Moeen Ali (captain)

My admiration for Mo has already been made clear, as have the reasons for my choosing him as captain of my team in white-ball cricket. His calmness under pressure, allied to his wide range of skills with both bat and ball, make him just about the perfect cricketer in this context. I think I'd choose him at the top of the order in white-ball cricket over any other player I've ever seen.

3. Phillip Hughes

On top of the many strengths Hughesy possessed in all forms of the game, his ability to score runs in his chosen areas regardless of field settings was simply phenomenal. I've lost count of the number of times I've seen him give himself room and penetrate the field behind square on the off side, even when two or three fielders had been placed to prevent exactly that. Unorthodox in some respects, he was just brilliant at building momentum in an innings in limited-overs cricket.

4. Graeme Hick

Hicky's inclusion in this side is beyond doubt. His record speaks for itself and I can only imagine the sort of clamour there would have been to obtain his services for the sort of franchise cricket which has characterised the modern game had he been around a few years longer.

5. Shakib Al Hasan

The inclusion of all-rounders in the white-ball game is something which I consider important and having a top-class slow left-armer like Shakib to call on makes a lot of sense to me. His ability to bowl at any stage in the innings from the first powerplay to the death overs always impressed me, and along with his destructive capability with the bat made him a valuable asset. Perhaps we didn't see the very best of him as a batsman during his time at New Road, but there was sufficient potential for me to pick him ahead of some of the other many candidates for a middle-order berth.

6. Ross Whiteley

As big hitters go, Ross is one of the very best I ever played with. It's easy to recall some of his fifties or sixties off 30 or 40 balls but what often gets overlooked is the number of occasions on which he contributed a rapid 15 or 20 from just a few deliveries and helped us reach sizeable totals. I think I'd rate him even higher than Hicky in terms of sheer ball striking, and as he's one of the finest fielders I've ever seen the decision to include him is an easy one.

7. Ben Cox

As a gloveman, Coxy is right up there with the best of them, and though I preferred Steven Davies in the longer format because of his slightly superior batting ability, in my white-ball side Ben gets the nod. With some talented spinners in this team, his excellence standing up to the stumps would be especially valuable. As he has regularly demonstrated in our more recent Twenty20 successes, his clever run-scoring, based on a mixture of power hitting, sweeps and neat deflections makes him a difficult man to bowl at, so he's an ideal man to have coming in at seven.

8. Chaminda Vaas

I considered a number of candidates for this spot in the side, including Andre Russell, Andrew Hall and Ed Barnard, but in the end, I opted for Chaminda for his versatility. He could swing the white ball early on in an innings and was an absolute master when it came to bowling yorkers in the later stages. I recall a team meeting when Tom Moody, as coach, was attempting to pick Chaminda's brains to help some of the other bowlers improve their death bowling. He asked Vaas whether he thought it best to be fractionally short or full when delivering yorkers and we were all slightly nonplussed when he stated almost nonchalantly that neither was an option. 'Just bowl proper yorkers,' he said, as though it was the easiest thing in the world to do. His occasionally explosive batting was another factor in my decision to include him.

9. Kabir Ali

In some ways a right-arm version of Chaminda, Kabir was another extremely skilful white-ball bowler. He offered very little width to the batsman and by altering his action slightly, opting for a low, slingy delivery, was another terrific exponent of the yorker. He was also capable of hitting the ball a long way and clearing the ropes, an important consideration for a lower-order batsman in the shorter formats. I often think Kabir was an underrated cricketer and he is another who might have enjoyed greater acclaim had his career been at its height just a few years later than it was.

10. Saeed Ajmal

Having a bowler within the side in limited-overs cricket who actually enjoys bowling in the final overs is a boon for any captain, and Saeed was one who genuinely thrived under that pressure. In the 2011 Twenty20 fixture against Northamptonshire at Milton Keynes, he took three wickets for no runs in the final over, a maiden, to finish with figures of 4-1-14-4 in what was the single most brilliant example of death bowling I ever witnessed. His selection is an easy one.

11. Pat Brown

Choosing Browny, a relative youth, in a selection of players made from my entire career might be something of a surprise, but his contribution to the improvement in our Twenty20 performances which went so far towards us gaining that big prize in 2018 was massive. I have previously commented upon the particular skills he brought to bear, and at his best I think he remains one of the cleverest exponents of his trade in that format.

That's out! I've just bowled Adam Wheater in the Blast final 2019

T20 semi-final 2019. Famous last words as Dan Christian tells Pat, 'Calm down, mate! We only need ten'.

Badsey Colts FC. Clue: I'm in the front row

Senior football for Bret as a teenager

With my son, Fred, at his first Villa game

At Wembley for Villa's League Cup Final in 2020 with my great mates, Radar and Muz

At a Team England golf day at The Grove in 2019

Ready to tee off with Ian Ward, Eoin Morgan and Matt Wheeler

At Disneyland Paris with the family

With the family, welcoming my new nephew in 2021

I always tried to help guide the youngsters! With Jack Haynes at Cheltenham races.

With Hughesy and the Phys (WCCC physio Ben Davies) at Bret in 2012

A timeless classic. The view across the New Road ground

New Road June 2007

Batting with Brian Lara for MCC at Lord's in 2014

With England selectors Ed Smith and James Taylor at Lord's in 2019. Possibly the nearest I ever got to the side!

What a shot (by the photographer not me) as I'm bowled by Finn Hudson-Prentice at Derby in 2021 [David Griffin]

The boy from Bret scrubs up well. Addressing the PCA Christmas Lunch at Lord's in 2019

Close of play

15

LOOKING FORWARD

THE ASHES defeat suffered by England in the winter of 2021/22 brought with it considerable negative criticism in the media. Questions were raised concerning preparation, selection, coaching and technique, especially that of the batsmen.

There was no question that, despite occasional bright spots, the team had performed badly, but a thorough consideration of the factors which might have affected performance levels is complicated. The picture was also clouded, in this particular case, by issues concerning the global pandemic and its impact on players' movement around the world, periods of isolation and a concern for their general welfare.

Most of the negative assessments, however, were not new. Critics of The Hundred glibly laid the blame for all the game's ills at its door; others pointed to the allure of franchises and some to the marginalisation of red-ball cricket in the domestic calendar. In my opinion, the reality is that within this complex conundrum there is some truth in all of those views, but there simply is no easy fix.

A large percentage of the professionals that I know still regard Test cricket as the ultimate measure of quality. If a player in the men's game has the requisite quality to reach that level and is prepared to invest the enormous amounts of effort and energy, both mental and physical, to make it, then he will be well-rewarded financially. So there is an incentive for a promising young red-ball cricketer to work hard and aim high.

Yet that same player might also be a skilful performer in the white-ball game. Here, he could attract the attention of those responsible for putting together franchise teams for The Hundred, the IPL, the Big Bash or one of the other competitions which take place across the world. The financial benefit of such recognition is likely to be high and considered as a ratio between time invested and monetary reward, the white-ball deal looks very attractive.

My point is that providing, of course, you are in possession of the requisite skills, it's just easier to be a wealthy white-ball cricketer, moving around the world plying your trade on different continents, than it is to be a Test regular.

My views mainly concern our domestic players, but I suspect the same is true for those from other Test-playing nations, some of which could be said to have struggled more than England with this so-called talent drain problem.

I stress that I am not suggesting that our young players just don't want to play Test cricket. I'm pretty sure that early on, the ultimate dream for most is a match-winning performance in an Ashes Test at Lord's, or something similar. But, whereas once that was almost the only truly meaningful pinnacle of a professional career, now there are several other options. And if the first and most traditional of those is also the toughest to achieve, it is inevitable that it will not necessarily be pursued hungrily by every player.

So we have young players who are aware that if they can sufficiently develop their white-ball skills they can earn relatively large sums of money in a short time. There might be a few who take the view that, in spite of the demands involved, they want to spend long hours honing their red-ball techniques in pursuit of the Test match dream, but even then, the likelihood is that, like me, they will want to be included in limited-overs cricket, too.

There are a lucky few, like Joe Root, Ben Stokes and Moeen, who have been blessed with the necessary abilities to play at the very top in all formats, but they are exceptional. As the amount of cricket played across the world grows, I wonder if it will become increasingly difficult to be such a player. Indeed, the very volume of cricket is an issue in itself which needs to be part of the conversation surrounding where the game is headed.

Nor can we ignore the changes which have taken place in society since Test cricket was in its halcyon days. A game which occupies five days does not especially recommend itself to life in a modern world where many consumers access highlights packages on mobile devices, and the popularity of shorter forms of the game underlines that.

Anyway, following the 2021/22 Ashes series, there was a feeling that some sort of reset was required in the domestic game to shift the focus back to red-ball cricket, and though not a unanimous view it was one which carried sufficient weight for it to occupy the minds of many of the game's administrators. In my role with the PCA, I was asked for my views as to how the domestic cricket calendar might best be rearranged. A brief outline of my thoughts goes some way to indicating the complexity of the issue.

It is my personal view that retaining the 18-county system is vital. County clubs are vitally important parts of their communities, and to deliberately remove any of them from the domestic structure would be wrong. The demise of several professional football clubs in England has demonstrated the negative impact of such losses on those to whom they mean a great deal. To effectively destroy institutions which have histories going back more than 150 years, would be to show a serious lack of respect for the clubs, their members, and players, past and present. Additionally, from a PCA perspective, the county clubs are the workplaces of those whom we represent, and any reduction in their numbers means we lose members, which is obviously not a desirable outcome.

To keep 18 counties, I believe we need to embrace The Hundred. Many of its fiercest initial critics eventually admitted that it was a huge success in its inaugural season and could be said to have achieved many of its targets. It did introduce cricket to a new audience, helped in no small part by being on free-to-air television, and its impact on the popularity of the women's game was immeasurable. Financially, its benefit to all the counties was, and will continue to be, absolutely vital. I attended a good number of games in the 2021 launch season and, quite unexpectedly to be honest, found that I was completely blown away by the spectacle, the atmospheres created and the general excitement generated.

The Twenty20 Blast is another vital source of revenue for the counties which must be protected, and finals day, as I have stressed via my own experiences as a player, has become the single biggest day of the domestic cricket calendar. It also represents the only opportunity for the bulk of the professional cohort to play a high-profile short form of the game.

We also need to retain a meaningful 50-over competition. Having worked so hard, and for so long, to win the World Cup in 2019, English cricket surely must maintain some degree of focus on this format. It is immensely popular with supporters of the counties and to many is the very definition of one-day cricket. Allowing a somewhat more considered and protracted approach to the white-ball game, it also tests some skills which the Blast and The Hundred don't necessarily address. If we continue down the route of our only 50-over cricket being a development competition, as it was in 2021, England's performances will eventually suffer, and the same arguments levelled at the game's administrators for the neglect of red-ball cricket following the Ashes defeat, will reappear about this format.

Another consideration when attempting to devise a workable calendar, is that it must create environments where the cricket is of the highest standard. This is the most likely way to bridge the gap between domestic and international cricket, and ultimately that is a primary aim. So, the maximum number of opportunities for the best to play against the best, on the best possible surfaces, must be facilitated, which impacts on the debate regarding the number of divisions in the Championship. It is also helpful if the schedule attracts more spectators.

Finally, as far as calendar cornerstones are concerned, comes the requirement to play a good proportion of four-day County Championship fixtures between May and August, when the weather is likely to be good, and pitches consequently up to standard.

Clearly, to achieve an outcome which takes into account all of the above is almost impossible. There must inevitably be compromises reached between the various stakeholders involved. A possible reduction in the number of Championship fixtures, perhaps made easier by the adoption of a three-division system, is one suggestion. Players being prepared to accept that separating the season into specific blocks of one format or another might not always be possible, necessitating a willingness to be more adaptable, is another. There are no easy solutions.

The need for our game to address racism has been brought into clear focus by the experiences of the former Yorkshire player, Azeem Rafiq, which came to everybody's attention at the end of 2021. The great former West Indian fast bowler, Michael Holding, eloquently highlighted 'unconscious bias' – the associations held by individuals outside their conscious awareness and control – in cricket and wider society. It certainly provided me with food for thought.

One of the realisations of which I have become aware is that whenever I consider this topic, I am seeing things from a white person's perspective. Rafiq's testimony has made many cricketers like me consider whether or not they have simply failed to notice wrongs which were happening around them. I feel fortunate that at Worcestershire we have, in my experience, always had individuals from black, Asian and minority ethnic (BAME) backgrounds in quite senior positions within the dressing room. But that does not mean that I dismiss the suggestion that I might have been guilty of unconscious bias or failing to understand what is termed white privilege.

County cricket has historically been dominated at all levels by white, male figures, from players to members and administrators. It is, therefore, inevitable that their views and thinking have dictated policy in all areas. Many such figures have at all times acted in good faith, never consciously and deliberately promoting inequality, but experiences highlighted by BAME cricketers, and those in wider society, clearly demonstrate the need for change. We need to examine our attitudes and actions in order to make it just as easy for an individual from any background to thrive in the game, in whatever capacity, as a white upper, or middle-class person.

The growth in popularity and the enormous improvements in standard of the women's game have also brought about a rethink regarding misogyny. Just as there have been neglectful attitudes towards BAME cricketers, the same is true of those towards females. A number of high-profile names have spoken of their experiences in this regard.

What is required is a clear determination to address the need for change in county cricket's attitudes towards all forms of discrimination. The PCA is keen to play its part in this process via its education programmes and I am hopeful that improvements are already underway. My personal belief is that we have reached a point where it is not just necessary for players to manage their own behaviour when it comes to these matters, but that they must feel able to call out any transgressions without fear. This obviously requires moral courage, but we will never right the wrongs which exist in the game unless this can happen.

Another area of the domestic game which many feel requires attention surrounds pathways into the professional arena. The plethora of privately educated players rising to the top of county cricket, and even into the England setup, is a cause for concern. This is not happening by chance. The high standard of cricket in these schools is undeniable and is a result of the outstanding facilities and coaching offered by many. The awarding of scholarships to promising state school pupils who transfer to these elite establishments only serves to reinforce their dominance.

At Worcestershire, we have benefited considerably from this situation in recent years. Whereas when I joined the academy programme, there were lads coming in from state schools in Redditch, Kidderminster and Evesham, most of our recent professional recruits have come from independent schools like Shrewsbury and Malvern College. A similar situation prevails at many other counties. The opportunity for elite coaches to spend considerable amounts of time with these privileged youngsters is enhanced by the fact that many of these schools are boarding institutions, meaning that the pupils are on site all the time, and therefore available for early morning or evening sessions.

Where does this leave a boy or girl who is at state school? Even if these youngsters become part of a county academy the amount of travelling to attend regular sessions can be a significant discouraging factor for players and parents. The expense involved might also be prohibitive. The former Sussex and England wicketkeeper, Matt Prior, has been an outspoken critic of a system which often requires parents to pay substantial amounts for coaching and equipment. It must surely be a priority for the professional game to ensure that young players are not priced out of inclusion.

My final point on this matter is a purely personal one. I have long held the view that we do not necessarily deploy our coaches appropriately when it comes to finding the best possible way to develop our young players. The elite coaches, those with the greatest knowledge of the game, generally tend to work with players who have already reached a good standard and are therefore less likely to benefit from their input. Logic dictates to me that we should have our best coaches involved lower down the pathway where their impact will be greater. What Rahul Dravid has achieved with the India Under-19 team is evidence to support my view.

Cricket, both domestically and internationally, clearly faces many challenges as my time as a player ends. Many of the issues I have raised are complex and multifaceted and I do not pretend to offer easily applied solutions to the game's problems. However, I do believe strongly that intelligent, thoughtful and responsible compromise can and will provide the game with a healthy future. I hope that I will be able to play my part in delivering that.

16

REFLECTIONS

THE COUNTY game I left was very different from the one that I entered, an inevitable observation since my involvement spanned over two decades. Looking back, it is interesting to reflect on the various changes that I experienced, some of them considerably bigger than others.

The behaviour of players was affected considerably by the introduction of 12-month contracts, which brought with them a greater responsibility for year-round fitness and significantly increased the opportunities for coaches to work with their charges. Whereas once we had a first XI coach, a second XI coach and a physiotherapist, the backroom staff at most clubs grew to include all of those, plus a bowling coach, several assistant coaches, possibly a fielding coach, an academy director, one or two strength and conditioning specialists, a sports psychologist and at least a couple of physios.

This transformed the daily work of players in a variety of ways; year-round training, increased emphasis on diet, gym work and lifestyle choices became the norm. Practice used to be very much based around the nets, and as a batsman you would face real bowlers on a frequent basis. I can hardly remember Tom Moody or Damian D'Oliveira ever bowling or throwing a ball.

The increased concern about bowlers' workloads saw that change, and you became almost as likely to face a coach throwing balls as an actual bowler. The use of the 'sidearm', or 'dog stick' as players call them, a plastic device used for propelling the ball at speed with very little effort, made this a lot easier.

The dog stick has become a key part of any coach's kitbag, a very common sight in most cricket nets and a valuable tool. I am a fan of its use in offering a batter the opportunity to hit lots of balls, but have some reservations regarding its effectiveness in helping develop footwork. Because the stick extends the arm of the thrower who is using it by about two feet, the bounce of the ball is generally steeper than would be the case with a simple throw. Consequently, the batter might find that in playing the ball, he is stuck in the crease somewhat, often unable to get forward, and if such practice is so frequent that this habit becomes ingrained, then problems can follow.

Another aspect of the dog stick which bothers some batters concerns the moment of release of the ball. When facing a conventional bowler, we all read a lot of cues, those little signs that help a batter to pick up the length of the ball, as the bowler gathers at the crease just prior to release. Of course, few of these are in evidence when the stick is used and reading the exact moment when the ball begins its downward trajectory is tricky. I know that Alastair Cook has worries about this, and prefers coaches to physically throw the ball at him without an artificial aid. There are frequent suggestions that modern batters get stuck on the crease too often, and this type of practice might possibly be a consideration. I suspect that, as in most areas, compromise will offer the most effective solution.

As a batter, the various chunks of willow I wielded over the years went through a process of evolution, and certainly those with which I played in latter seasons were quite different in both feel and performance from their predecessors. As a young player, I would often pinch a bat from a senior, as they always tended to have the choicest blades, but the rookies in the dressing room as my career was drawing to a close seemed to be well-supplied.

The modern bat has a much larger profile than used to be the case and you only need to watch a Twenty20 game, at almost any level, to appreciate how well they can dispatch the ball if in the right hands. The size of some of the bats I saw over the years, especially the thickness of the edges, was almost ridiculous, and it was right that the MCC brought in restrictions in 2017. One particular monster of a bat I recall was used by Steffan Jones when he played for Derbyshire against us at New Road as far back as 2010. He made 86 in the first innings, batting at number 11, and smashed 15 fours and a six with a piece of wood like a railway sleeper.

I never chose especially big bats but those I favoured as I became more experienced, were probably pressed slightly less than previously, and consequently performed better but were not as robust. It is generally true that bats break more easily now than they used to, and there are various suggestions as to why, including considerations of willow density and moisture content. What I would say categorically is that one thing certainly hasn't changed – it's not the bat that matters but the player who's holding it.

Analysis of the game, facilitated by the technological advances which have occurred since I started playing, has become an important component of a county coach's work and of team preparation generally. Every ball of every game is now viewed and logged by a dedicated team of experts, and all the collected data is more or less available at the click of a mouse. It's easy for a player to watch his own performances, and those of opponents, to make technical adjustments or to plan for future encounters. Pre-match team meetings are supported by video and statistical evidence, and coaches can send packages of information to players' laptops or phones.

There are legitimate questions asked by some of the game's followers about the effectiveness of such forensic investigation, and some cynics assert that they don't necessarily see an enormous improvement in performance as a result. However, what has to be remembered is that this examination of players' strengths and weaknesses is available to all teams, so just as one side's bowlers are targeting the perceived weaknesses of the other's batters, exactly the same process is taking place in reverse. Arguably, the net result is that the two forces cancel each other out. But if one side were to discard the opportunity to use data analysis, the chances are it would suffer in direct contests with opponents who did use it.

Let me clarify. In preparation for a Twenty20 game, for example, I might receive information from our analyst telling me that a certain right-handed batter favoured the reverse sweep. When bowling to him I might normally have only a single fielder behind square on the off side, enabling me to have a midwicket inside the fielding circle, where I was most likely to be hit. Knowing that he was likely to reverse me, however, I could place two fielders behind square on the off side. Sometimes, the detail might be as specific as to suggest that such a player will reverse sweep, but not until he has faced at least ten balls, enabling an even more targeted field alteration. If he caught me out by doing it before that, I would, of course, blame the analyst!

Another scenario might involve being shown how a particular bowler always responds to being struck for a boundary by bowling a slower ball or a bouncer next up, meaning that we knew what was likely to be coming, which, essentially, encapsulates the whole aim of the employment of this kind of analysis – being in possession of some idea of what's coming next. One-day cricket is no longer just about playing it off the cuff, and all professional outfits are using whatever data is available to them in order to maximise their chances of success.

In the time-honoured debate about improving or declining standards in county cricket, one area tends never to divide opinion. It is surely beyond doubt that the quality of fielding in the game has never been higher, and that is a direct consequence of the impact of the white-ball, and especially Twenty20, format. By the time I started, the days of the odd, slow, lumbering passenger in the field had already passed, but I still witnessed a steady development of fielding skills as my career progressed. The fleetness of foot, willingness to dive and slide, and the accuracy of throw of almost every fielder improved year on year, while breathtaking boundary catches, often involving a release then a recatch by the same fielder, have become almost commonplace. There were always a few outstanding fielders, but by the time I departed the playing scene, it was those that were not of high quality who were the exceptions.

The actual process of batting, particularly at the top of the order in first-class cricket, has, I think, become more difficult since I started. Whilst the fundamentals of batting which I tried to observe throughout my career have remained the same, the methods adopted by bowlers have moved on. My advice to any young batter has always been to keep things as simple as possible, to make sure your head is still at the point of delivery, regardless of whatever trigger movement you adopt, and to watch the ball as closely as possible. Changing guard from the conventional middle or middle-and-leg options, sometimes even batting on off stump, is something which became popular towards the end of my career and though I tried different guards at various times I tended to revert back to a more conventional approach most of the time. Batting on off stump can help a batter to leave the ball but also makes them more vulnerable to the possibility of being dismissed lbw if the ball moves back in.

The growing propensity of top-class pace bowlers to adopt a 'wobble seam' approach, which became almost the norm in the last few years of my time, has certainly made leaving the ball more difficult, and is often overlooked when critics vilify modern players. What this method does is allow bowlers to eschew the traditional approach of adopting a straightforward policy of striving to swing or seam the ball one way or the other, and to bowl deliveries which could go either way off the pitch. If even the bowler doesn't know which way it's going to move, then clearly the batter is at a distinct disadvantage. Whereas once it was possible for an experienced opener to look at a bowler's grip and be fairly certain of what to expect, it became far more a matter of guesswork. In some respects, I feel this is one of the reasons for the demise of the traditional swing bowler, once a staple in almost any county or league team.

A consequence of this is that on flat pitches which offer little in the way of movement, bowlers have found their penetration limited, whereas a genuine swing bowler might have been effective whatever the surface. Along with the improvement in bats, and the increased likelihood of batters to attempt to dominate, owing to their having played a great deal more white-ball cricket, the contest between bat and ball has become somewhat different from how it was 10 or 20 years ago. All of which is a perfectly acceptable, and indeed welcome, indication that cricket continues to change and develop with time; surely part of the game's enduring appeal.

Whether or not players' skills improved in all aspects of the game during my time will always be a question which divides opinion. Every disappointing performance by an England Test team raises questions regarding batting technique. This is an area of concern for coaches, but there surely can't be many who don't accept that batting in limited-overs formats has got better. The range of shots produced in white-ball cricket has grown hugely and has without doubt enhanced the spectacle.

Travelling will always be a part of a county cricketer's lot and is another area where things have moved on. Players' sponsored cars, often emblazoned with their name and credentials, are a thing of the past, and are no longer to be seen cruising up and down the motorways. At least this has spared me the sort of embarrassment once suffered by former Worcestershire opener, Tim Curtis, a player with whom Bumpy often compared me. He once returned to his sponsored Volvo to find that someone had etched a message into the dirt on the boot which read '0-60 in 3 days'!

Most teams now travel by coach, and from a health and safety perspective this can only be a good thing. The idea of playing a four-day game in, say, Scarborough, and then driving to Canterbury late at night, for a fixture the following day, now seems laughable, whereas at one time it was quite common. Some veterans might bemoan the change, as it has removed the opportunity to bump up their expenses, but even they will readily admit that coach travel is safer. The time a group spends travelling together also improves the team bonding process, a useful and underestimated benefit.

There is far less county cricket played on outgrounds than was the case in the early part of my career, and though this is justifiably mourned by those who enjoyed sitting in sun-drenched deckchairs at places like Eastbourne, Arundel and Abergavenny, I can't claim to miss them quite as much. Although Colwyn Bay will always be special to me for obvious reasons, and I regularly enjoyed success at the beautiful Cheltenham College ground, I generally preferred the more luxurious facilities of the established county bases, where practice facilities, changing accommodation and catering tended to be better.

As well as playing alongside many great talents, it was obviously a thrill and an honour to be in direct opposition to some of the very best cricketers, not only of my lifetime but in the game's history. Having pitted my wits and tested my skills at various times against Shane Warne, Muttiah Muralitharan, Anil Kumble and Mushtaq Ahmed, I can claim to have genuine first-hand experience of some of the world's greatest spin bowlers. Sadly I only faced Warney for a couple of overs, against Hampshire at Kidderminster in 2007, before falling to Shaun Udal at the other end, but at least I can say he didn't get me out. And whilst I have huge respect for the countless dedicated and skilful cricketers of the county game who challenged me, entertained me and amused me in the hundreds of appearances I made for the Pears, inevitably certain individuals stand out. England greats Jimmy Anderson and Stuart Broad have presented regular challenges – I've tended to fare rather better against the latter – and Dale Steyn was also a formidable adversary amongst the quicks.

As for the batsmen I've admired, Sir Alastair Cook stands out, and I count myself very lucky to have got to know him quite well, particularly when I shared a room with him for a couple of weeks on an MCC tour in Abu Dhabi. Kumar Sangakkara, the Sri Lankan genius, is another with whom I feel blessed to have been able to share a pitch, and then there is Brian Lara. When I found myself in the same team as the West Indian legend, it is probably the only occasion on which I have ever felt genuinely star-struck.

The occasion was a game at Lord's in June 2014 which formed part of the bicentennial celebrations of cricket at the game's most famous ground. I was selected to play in the same MCC team as Brian, against Hertfordshire, in a repeat of the first fixture ever played there in 1814. Having grown up watching Lara on television and feeding on a diet of the legendary 'Brian Lara Cricket' computer game, to actually bat with him at Headquarters was an unforgettable experience. It was a 40-over affair and having picked up a couple of wickets in the Hertfordshire innings, I opened the batting as we chased a target of 199. Knowing that the great man was to bat at number three, both I and my opening partner, our skipper, Jonathan Wileman, a useful Minor Counties player who played a few games for Nottinghamshire in the early 90s, were keen to partner him. There was a subtle suggestion that one of us should do the decent thing and give up our wicket so that Lara was guaranteed to bat but, not surprisingly, neither of us was particularly inclined to make the sacrifice.

Eventually, after an opening stand of 104, Jonathan was dismissed for 67 and my dream of batting with one of the absolute all-time greats was realised. In his company, I passed the half-century mark and we shared a 65-run partnership before I was stumped for 64. The photographs I still have of the occasion, including one of the scoreboard displaying both of our names, are among my most treasured memorabilia.

That's one particularly special memory and there are various personal achievements which are sources of satisfaction. Carrying my bat on four occasions and making a hundred in both innings of a Championship match the same number of times, are noteworthy, as is the fact that in 225 first-class matches I never suffered the indignity of bagging a pair.

On many occasions I have heard, and even used, the expression that cricket is only a game. However, I believe that to be only partly true. That it is a game, something which is engaged in for fun, is undeniable and, as I stressed when discussing the restart of county proceedings in 2020 following the pandemic lockdown, even professionals recognise as much. For me, though, and for many thousands of others, it is far more.

How a recreation which began in the Middle Ages when a few people started hitting a ball with a stick, has come to be the defining centrepiece of my own existence is difficult to put into words. Not only have I earned a living and been able to provide for my family thanks to cricket, but it has shaped my character, my personality and my everyday life. I owe almost everything I am, and all that I stand for, to the game and its values.

Underpinning that assessment has been my enduring affiliation to Worcestershire County Cricket Club.

I will forever be grateful that I was once a Pear.

STATISTICS

First-Class Career 2005-21

Batting and Fielding

M	I	NO	Runs	HS	Ave	100	50	Ct
225	403	40	13,920	298	38.34	39	55	301

Bowling

O	M	R	W	BB	Ave
548.1	96	1,649	33	4-49	49.96

Centuries

Date	Venue	Opposition	Score
			(for Worcestershire)
August 2006	Colwyn Bay	Glamorgan	134*
April 2007	Worcester	L'boro UCCE	112
Aug 2008	Colchester	Essex	102
April 2009	Oxford	Oxford UCCE	140*

Sept 2009	Taunton	Somerset	298
May 2010	Worcester	Derbyshire	148
Aug 2010	Cheltenham	Gloucestershire	104 (1st inns)
			134* (2nd inns)
Aug 2010	Colwyn Bay	Glamorgan	165*
April 2012	Nottingham	Notts	102
Aug 2012	Worcester	Middlesex	133*
May 2013	Oxford	Oxford MCCU	118
May 2013	Worcester	Essex	156
April 2014	Southampton	Hampshire	172*
May 2014	Cardiff	Glamorgan	109 (1st inns)
			151* (2nd inns)
June 2014	Leicester	Leicestershire	120
July 2014	Cheltenham	Gloucestershire	167*
May 2015	Southampton	Hampshire	142*
July 2015	Worcester	Hampshire	206*
March 2016	Oxford	Oxford MCCU	155
Aug 2016	Worcester	Northants	107* (1st inns)
			103 (2nd inns)
May 2017	Derby	Derbyshire	120
May 2017	Northampton	Northants	161
June 2017	Hove	Sussex	121
June 2017	Worcester	Kent	142
Aug 2017	Worcester	Gloucestershire	130
Sept 2017	Nottingham	Notts	139*
Sept 2017	Worcester	Durham	123*

June 2018	Worcester	Lancashire	118 (1st inns)
			163 (2nd inns)
Aug 2018	Scarborough	Yorkshire	178
Sept 2018	Worcester	Yorkshire	127
April 2019	Leicester	Leicestershire	114
Sept 2019	Worcester	Glamorgan	139
Aug 2020	Worcester	Warwickshire	110
July 2021	Worcester	Warwickshire	113
		(for Mountaineers)	
Feb 2012	Mutare	Mid West Rhinos	178

Carried bat through entire innings

Date	Venue	Opposition	Score	Total
Sept 2007	Hove	Sussex	70*	213
Aug 2012	Worcester	Middlesex	133*	323
July 2014	Cheltenham	Gloucestershire	167*	395
July 2015	Worcester	Hampshire	206*	478

List A Career 2005–19

Batting and Fielding

M	I	NO	Runs	HS	Ave	100	50	S/R	Ct
135	120	17	3,466	107	33.65	4	22	81.93	56

Bowling

O	M	R	W	BB	Ave	Econ
530.1	3	2,925	81	4-19	36.11	5.51

Centuries

Date	Venue	Opposition	Score
May 2013	Hove	Sussex	107
Aug 2013	Worcester	Bangladesh A	101
May 2018	Worcester	Lancashire	102*
April 2019	Manchester	Lancashire	101

Twenty20 Career 2005–21

Batting and Fielding

M	I	NO	Runs	HS	Ave	100	50	S/R	Ct
177	135	34	2,310	68*	22.87	0	7	118.88	74

Bowling

O	M	R	W	BB	Ave	Econ
390.1	1	2,999	101	5-28	29.69	7.68

Player-of-the-Match awards

July 2007 T20 v Warwickshire (a)	DNB		3-0-18-3
July 2012 T20 v Gloucestershire (a)	31	(13b)	3-0-26-2
June 2014 T20 v Leicestershire (a)	67*	(50b)	4-0-26-1
June 2014 T20 v Warwickshire (h)	62*	(45b)	2-0-15-0
May 2015 T20 v Leicestershire (h)	58	(47b)	4-0-13-1
June 2015 T20 v Durham (a)	56	(49b)	3-0-23-2
June 2015 T20 v Lancashire (a)	53	(40b)	1-0-8-0

ACKNOWLEDGEMENTS

I MUST admit, when I was first approached about writing an autobiography, my initial reaction was to ask who would really want to read what I have to say? Perhaps in that moment, I underestimated the passion that people have for county cricket, and maybe I took for granted a game that has shaped my life and will continue to do so.

I have lived a boyhood dream of representing my home county, and earning a living from the sport I love, for the best part of two decades. Just maybe there is a reasonable story to tell. There's certainly been a lot of laughs, and a few tears, along the way.

The process of putting together this book has enabled me to rediscover some fabulous memories. It has been both humbling and therapeutic, and I am extremely thankful for the journey I've been on. I'd like to thank all my team-mates, coaches, opponents, officials and administrators, for being part of our great game and my experiences. A special mention to all of the Worcestershire members and supporters for their unwavering backing over the years. Having been one of your own on the field, I'm looking forward to being a very excitable one of your number, getting behind the lads in the summer of 2022 and beyond.

I'd like to say a huge thank you to Frank Watson for all of the help, research and sheer bloody hard work put into the writing of this book, and, of course, to 'Super Mo', as my son Freddie calls him, for penning the foreword. Thanks also to all at Pitch Publishing, and I know Frank wants to express his appreciation to Dave Bradley, John Curtis, John Weston, Tim Jones and Mark Cripps.

Finally, the biggest thank you to my friends, all at the Bughut, and my family, for all their support over the years from childhood to retirement. To Mum, Dad, Gran and Kate, thanks for the advice, for putting up with my obsession, the endless balls thrown and fetched in the garden and the countless journeys to and from matches. To my wife, Danni, and amazing kids, Freddie and Ava, thanks for all the love, sacrifice and understanding. I love you!

Mitch